FEMININE
INSPIRED LEADERSHIP

Power redefined. Leadership reimagined.

NICOLE VAN KUPPEVELD, MBA

© 2025 ALL RIGHTS RESERVED.

Published by She Rises Studios Publishing **www.SheRisesStudios.com**.

No part of this book may be reproduced or transmitted in any form whatsoever, electronic, or mechanical, including photocopying, recording, or by any informational storage or retrieval system without the expressed written, dated and signed permission from the publisher and author.

LIMITS OF LIABILITY/DISCLAIMER OF WARRANTY:

The author and publisher of this book have used their best efforts in preparing this material. While every attempt has been made to verify the information provided in this book, neither the author nor the publisher assumes any responsibility for any errors, omissions, or inaccuracies.

The author and publisher make no representation or warranties with respect to the accuracy, applicability, or completeness of the contents of this book. They disclaim any warranties (expressed or implied), merchantability, or for any purpose. The author and publisher shall in no event be held liable for any loss or other damages, including but not limited to special, incidental, consequential, or other damages.

ISBN: 978-1-966798-72-9

Dedication

To my dad, Andre Gerard Guay,

who embodied the spirit of feminine-inspired leadership in our home, in community, and through his work as General Manager at Lafarge Canada Ltd. in Edmonton. Reminding me that authentic leadership is focused on people, purpose and passion, where success is not measured solely by personal financial gain, but by the meaningful impact that as leaders we can make in our teams, organizations and in the world.

Always with me, Dad.

Table of Contents

Advanced Reader Reviews 7

Preface 11

Welcome: A Personal Invitation to Lead Differently 18

Chapter 1: Why We Need a Feminine Reimagining of Leadership 23

Chapter 2: Leading with Values That Fit — Personal, Team and
    Organizational 32

Chapter 3: Trust Is Your Leadership Currency 42

Chapter 4: Communication That Connects —
    Even When It's Tough 54

Chapter 5: Learning Together — Growing Into Teams That Thrive 71

Chapter 6: Thinking Way Beyond Black and White 84

Chapter 7: Relationship Intelligence — Leading Through
    Connection, Not Control 96

Chapter 8: Leading Through Change and Transition 109

Chapter 9: Leading the Feminine- Inspired Way 125

Appendix A: Resource Toolkits 130

Appendix B: Feminine-Inspired Case Studies & Stories 147

About the Author 184

Advanced Reader Reviews

In an era where leadership trends often feel like fleeting buzzwords, *Feminine-Inspired Leadership* stands out as a lasting, practical approach that leaders can actually use. Nicole doesn't just talk about leading through change—she equips you with the mindset, tools and processes to make it happen in real, day-to-day leadership moments.

What struck me most was how seamlessly she connects performance with human connection. By blending empathy, curiosity and clear direction, her approach creates an environment where both people and performance thrive — not as competing priorities but as partners in success.

Whether you're navigating complex organizational shifts, trying to strengthen your team's collaboration, or simply looking for a better way to lead, Nicole's insights will challenge you to rethink the "how" of leadership and inspire you to take action that matters. This isn't theory — *Feminine-Inspired Leadership* is a guide for real-world impact.
—**Tanner Chambers, Director, Social Enterprise and Environmental Sustainability, Bissell Centre**

* * *

In today's workplace, employees often feel uncertain about their organizations, frustrated by inconsistencies and wary of leadership intentions. Now more than ever, there's a desperate need for leaders to create environments and cultures that evolve with the ever-changing demands of the modern world.

That's where feminine-inspired leadership excels!

Nicole has a remarkable ability to embrace complex change and break it down into simple, actionable steps that engage employees instead of telling them. If your organization is ready to elevate its workplace culture and adopt an 'outside-the-box' approach to leadership, I highly recommend Nicole's!

—**Sarah Shaffer, Owner, Be A Butterfly,**
Life Strategy Coaching Be A Butterfly, LLC Life Strategy Coach

* * *

In a world built on mantras such as "It's just business" and "The end justifies the means," it is refreshing to engage with content centred on humanity. *Feminine-Inspired Leadership* offers simple yet actionable tools that serve as a roadmap for approaching our teams and organizations in a positive and collaborative manner. Reading it felt like small bursts of inspiration and reassurance that, through intentional leadership changes, it's possible to not only survive but thrive in modern society.

—**Devin Sarno, Founder of Parlay Communicators**
www.parlaycommunicators.com

* * *

This book is heartfelt and filled with lived wisdom. The author clearly poured her experience, insight and values into every chapter, and it shows. The feminine-inspired leadership framework is timely, meaningful and needed, and Nicole's voice as a guide feels credible, warm, and well-earned.

—**Kat Spencer, NirvanaonEarth.com**

* * *

In this book, Nicole van Kuppeveld elevates the qualities often dismissed as "soft" skills by situating them in the framework of feminine-inspired leadership. Reading it will give you insight into each leadership quality as well as the synergistic way they all fit together — you'll see why the whole truly is greater than the sum of its parts. If you've ever had a gut feeling about a better way to do things but couldn't explain why it would work, this book provides the rationale you've been missing.

—Rie Algeo Gilsdorf, Founder & Facilitator,
Embody Equity Embody Equity

* * *

Feminine-Inspired Leadership is a book that every leader needs to read regardless of gender or length of leadership tenure.

The concepts and strategies that Nicole describes have been used and modelled by Nicole in her work as a successful leadership consultant to facilitate growth in others. These well-described and practical strategies have been proven to create dynamic shifts in leadership mindsets and approaches, and help to create strong, healthy organizations with employees who are highly engaged, thriving and productive.

This book highlights that as a leader, our biggest assets are our employees and if we can engage authentically and lead with empathy, intuition and collaboration, we will strengthen individuals and teams. Through applying what you learn from this book, you will be able to provide other organizational leaders and employees with tools and new ways of thinking and learning to achieve organizational vision and goals.

As I read *Feminine-Inspired Leadership*, I felt Nicole's passion for sharing her wisdom and her compassion for leaders who find themselves in need of new ways to hold positional power and empower others. It is because Nicole understands the complex world of leadership today, that this book is relevant, timely and necessary for every leader to read to be successful in today's fast-paced and changing world!

—Karen Caine, Retired Social Worker and Not for Profit Leader

* * *

I read *Feminine-Inspired Leadership* in one sitting, it's that practical and engaging. As a master's student, I found it incredibly useful for understanding what future leadership looks like and its importance. Each chapter is like a go-to guide you can return to whenever you're stuck. I especially loved the emphasis on 'power to' vs. 'power over' and the clarity around values, perspective and communication. It's a must-read for anyone navigating leadership with empathy and impact.

—**Shruti Bairagi, Marketing Master's Student and Marketing Lead at Organizations by Design Inc.**

* * *

Nicole has written a great book with an easy and clear style. The content will aid CEOs, seasoned leaders or anyone considering a leadership role. *Feminine-Inspired Leadership* would have been an immense help to me during my professional career in my leadership roles.

—**Nancy BeasleyHosker, Retired Journalist and Communications Professional**

Preface

The world is in desperate need of transformative leadership.

It's time to rethink what makes a great leader. In my work as a leadership architect, I see over and over the need for forward-thinking business leaders to have a practical approach to navigating through challenges and complexities. If you are looking for a way to not just survive but thrive in leading your team, if you want to find proven tools and resources, then this leadership book is for you!

This feminine-inspired leadership approach focuses on knowing how to empower leaders to create psychologically safe workspaces where individuals feel valued, respected and inspired to contribute their best. It allows you to build collaborative learning teams and to cultivate this kind of leadership capacity at all levels of an organization. It may sound simple but it's not. However, not to worry, we will unpack it together.

This is the kind of book you can use at any point on your leadership journey, depending on your most pressing issue of the day. It's a practical guide filled with tools, techniques, stories, resources, reflective questions and case studies that you can come back to reference at any time. It's for leaders who want 'how to' tools, strategies and tried-and-true methods of getting to their desired outcomes and shared vision.

Building and finding our foundation

Thank you for choosing this book. As you and I both know, there are a bunch of books, theories, models and frameworks on leadership, a great many of which I've consumed over the years.

Good leadership is not about adhering to a rigid set of rules or predefined strategies. It's about cultivating your agility and resourcefulness to navigate the complexities of real-world challenges with confidence and clarity. Effective leadership lies in the cultivation of a growth mindset, team learning and reflective practice within your team and organizations. Leaders who want to grow need to engage in critical thinking, to learn from mistakes and to embrace diversity as a catalyst for ongoing growth.

My philosophy of feminine-inspired leadership is rooted in the principles of organizational learning, a concept championed by influential scholars in organizational learning and development such as Dr. Edgar Schein and Dr. Peter Senge. They believe that organizations learn, grow and evolve only if the individuals within are continuously learning from experiences as well as concepts. According to Senge, the ability to cultivate a learning organization — one that encourages experimentation, collaboration and knowledge sharing — is paramount in driving sustained success in today's business landscape.

In my experience leading many teams over two decades, organizational learning and a true commitment to human empowerment, growth and development are at the heart of effective leadership. It's about harnessing the full capacity of individuals, fostering a culture of trust and collaboration, and empowering employees to take ownership of their work and contribute meaningfully to organizational goals.

I invite you to embark on a journey of self-discovery and growth, to embrace the multi-faceted tapestry of leadership, recognizing that there is no one-size-fits-all approach. I encourage you to bring your authentic self to your leadership role, and a commitment to make a difference as a leader of your team, organization, sector, industry or community.

Why this matters to me

If you are curious about why this matters so much to me, it comes from a desire to help create workplaces where people feel supported, valued and motivated, and they learn every day. Most of us spend more than half our waking hours at work. We say that people are our greatest assets, but do we always treat them that way?

I am the founding partner of Organizations by Design Inc., based in Alberta, Canada. We provide leadership development and coaching services for leaders like you and your teams. The feminine-inspired framework I have developed has been curated over three decades of working for leaders, being a leader myself and training leaders.

I first became passionate about fixing toxic workplaces when I was a young occupational therapist working for a vocational rehabilitation organization, where I counselled people who were off work on stress leave. Over 10 years in that job I counselled more than 1,000 people. I figured out that it was not just their workplaces that were making these individuals sick. Their bosses also played a significant role in their medical leave, stress and burnout as well — or more specifically, their bosses' leadership styles and/or lack of leadership training.

My counselling role with these individual clients included meeting with their employers to gather a history of their on-the-job performance to better understand the issues each individual employee had in the workplace. Over the course of these interviews, over that decade, a pattern started to emerge. Not only were my clients sick, but there were harmful things happening in their workplaces that were contributing to their poor health. These things were directly related to how employees were managed and the unhealthy organizational cultures in which they were working.

The most disturbing repetitive pattern I saw in these workplaces was the complete absence of people-management skills. The employers' responses to my questions that addressed this area of leadership flabbergasted me. Surely, no human leading humans could think it was all right to say the kinds of things, in the ways they said them, to the people purported to be their greatest asset, could they? Not only did they say them, but they had little or no awareness of the impact they had, not only on my clients but their entire teams.

I was curious, so I started to ask another question as part of my assessment, and the answers were consistent: "I have had no leadership development training" or "I am really good at my job, but have no experience or expertise in managing teams of people." They reported that either their organizations did not have a budget for leadership training or they did not see it as a priority or they subscribed to the 'throw them in the deep end and see if they can swim' philosophy. As a result, these managers often felt they had indeed been thrown in the deep end, were isolated, had no resources and were forced to figure this 'managing people thing' out themselves. Many of them, very competent in the technical aspect of their work or other aspects of their leadership roles, felt like they were drowning when it came to providing leadership to their people.

Learning to be a leader myself

That decade as a counsellor was a learning laboratory in leadership and the impact that lack of leadership development can have on the confidence of individual managers. Over the next two decades I became a leader myself in a variety of capacities. I was a group psychotherapist. I led program teams in mental health at an agency. Then, at the provincial (state) level, I became a program director, leading a health portfolio that included four youth treatment facilities and a multi-million-dollar federal grant. Later, I was executive director of a provincial advocacy group, leading leaders. Then, I became manager of academic administration, working in the executive suite, at a local community college. I was the area director of a home health agency. And my last position, prior to opening my leadership consultancy, was as a member of an executive team leading a province-wide change initiative.

In the trenches I learned good leadership from great leaders, and how not to lead from a few horrible bosses. Along this journey I consulted the best leadership sources, like the *Harvard Business Review,* and integrated them into my own leadership style.

A significant experience was my Master of Business Administration (MBA) at Royal Roads University in Victoria, Canada, with a specialization in leadership and organizational behaviour. It was 2006, well into my professional career, and I was ready to acquire knowledge and some missing pieces about the makings of great leadership. I wanted to learn about the best qualities in one's leadership style, how to create the best teams and the conditions that enabled them to do their best work.

I applied that learning to my leadership roles and then moved from being a leader of teams to going into organizations as an organizational development consultant. This allowed me to take a deeper dive. To see whole organizations and the impact of leadership – on all stakeholders, especially their most valuable resources, their employees. This was another research laboratory to hone the art and science of humanistic leadership. During that time, I attended hundreds of seminars and workshops and obtained two certificates.

Organizations by Design Inc is born

In 2019, I decided to dedicate myself full-time to working with clients who were forward-thinking and wanting to learn a proven practical approach to leadership that would allow them to navigate in our increasingly complex world. And so Organizations by Design Inc. was formed. We learned valuable lessons through COVID about how to deliver engaging, impactful learning experiences for leaders in a highly interactive online environment. We are expanding beyond our humble beginnings and moving into international markets, offering feminine-inspired leadership development live online and through immersive leadership retreats around the world.

We aim in our work with clients and in this book to offer practical, actionable advice that you can implement immediately, whether you're facing a specific issue or simply looking to enhance your leadership skills. Let's dismiss the misconception that you either have leadership skills or you don't. Leadership is a skill that must be continuously refined through the lessons that we learn. High-value leadership development is not a soft skill. High-quality leadership development has a high return on investment and on your bottom line. This includes lower turnover, higher job satisfaction and engagement, lower absenteeism, innovation, high productivity, enhanced performance and high impact results.

The leadership approach you may be seeking

I wrote this book for those who seek a different approach to leadership — one focused on people, purpose and authenticity, where success is not measured solely by personal financial gain, but by the meaningful impact they make in the world. The book is for leaders who want to build collaborative learning teams and create workspaces where their employees say: "Hip hip hooray, we get to go to work today."

The environment in which we work is continuously evolving and will change exponentially in the next decade. In this new environment, there is a need for leaders who know how to leverage diversity, tap into the employees' collective wisdom and create collaboration that leverages stakeholder assets, internally and externally. Why? So that they can stay ahead of their competitors. So they can not just survive, but thrive.

Leadership is not about having all the answers — it's about creating the conditions for others to thrive. A lack of leadership clarity can lead to confusion, disengagement and burnout. And this can have a profound impact on your team. Defining your leadership philosophy and honing your skills through an applied approach like feminine-inspired leadership is the key to overcoming these challenges and achieving sustainable success.

If you're a leader who feels overwhelmed, stuck or unsure how to navigate the complexities of leading your team, now is the time to take action. The feminine-inspired framework will give you the tools, strategies and support you need to refine your leadership, build high-performing teams and create a thriving culture in your organization.

Are you ready to invest in yourself and your team? If you build your capacity as a leader by applying the practical tools, strategies and frameworks in this book you can change how you lead your teams, your organization and perhaps the world!

WELCOME

A Personal Invitation to Lead Differently

The next leg of your amazing leadership learning journey is about to begin.

Are you an aspiring leader or someone guiding future leaders, seeking a breakthrough way to develop the skills necessary to thrive in today's rapidly changing work environments?

If so, the feminine-inspired leadership framework offers a fresh approach to leading people that breaks away from one-size-fits-all models. It's designed with practicality in mind, giving you the "how-to" strategies needed to lead teams in today's complex, diverse and unpredictable environments.

This leadership book is a practical guide to leading with integrity, fostering learning environments and developing other people. It empowers leaders to embrace experiential learning and collaborative team dynamics and to build workspaces where people thrive.

A leadership approach for all

Unlike some leadership books that focus solely on theory, this book about feminine-inspired leadership blends real stories, practical tools and interactive exercises. You'll learn from leaders across industries who navigated challenges, grew through tough moments and emerged stronger. They are stories about my clients and their lessons are universal and impactful.

This book engages you directly, prompting critical thinking, self-reflection and a proven approach to developing yourself as a leader. I'll teach you how to apply a learning approach to deepen your leadership capacity, which you can apply today.

This approach is not just for women leaders. There are plenty of men who espouse this leadership philosophy — my father, a former General Manager at Lafarge Canada Ltd., was one of them. And I have had the privilege of learning from both women and men about how to integrate this framework into my leadership. The premise is that if you infuse your leadership with this feminine paradigm, while balancing some of the masculine paradigm in each situation you find yourself in as a leader, you'll be capable of leading through any challenge you face.

Engaging, practical and grounded in real-world application

Leadership isn't about just acquiring knowledge; it's about applying it. You'll learn to tackle real-world challenges through this book, not just get abstract advice.

The feminine-inspired leadership approach addresses challenging areas that leaders, like you, have struggled to resolve. Each chapter provides you with a practical proven path through these challenges. I offer solutions based on curated leading-edge leadership research that allows you to integrate the learning into your practice immediately, getting you the results you desire. This book will challenge you to think critically, engage thoughtfully and lead with confidence through areas that people leaders struggle with daily.

The core themes — authenticity, learning, engagement, diversity, thinking and integrity — will help you view leadership as an evolving journey, not a destination.

A resource toolbox for forward-thinking leaders

As a thought leader and researcher with 20 plus years of leadership experience, I've compiled a toolbox with cutting-edge resources, methodologies and perspectives in this book. Where you see text written in bold and underlined you will find further information in a resource section organized by chapter at the back of the book.

I have listed my go-to tools to allow you quick access, so you can use them right away. Whether you're dealing with change, mentoring new leaders or building team engagement, you'll find actionable tools to apply immediately. The intent is to help you create learning teams, an organizational culture and communities that drive long-term success.

In today's world, leaders must be agile, empathetic and constantly evolving. This book will help you thrive in your leadership role.

People leader key takeaways

This book is for people leaders at every level, from new leaders to seasoned managers seeking a fresh approach to leading diverse teams in today's array of workspaces. It's especially useful if other leadership methods aren't meeting the challenges you face in today's workplace environments.

It's ideal for new leaders wanting to make a deeper impact, managers aiming to better engage their teams and consultants or coaches looking for innovative leadership development strategies.

After reading this book, these will be your takeaways:

- **A fresh approach to leadership**: Embrace a process-based, actionable, experiential learning model that you can implement right away.

- **Real-world storytelling:** Leadership lessons brought to life through real examples, from real clients, with real leadership challenges that they have resolved.
- **Interactive and practical:** Tools, resources and exercises you can apply immediately, including some case studies based on my clients — leaders like you.
- **A holistic leadership framework**: Integrate learning, systems thinking and psychological safety into your practice.
- **Coaching and mentoring tools**: Strategies for self-development and team leadership so you can grow yourself and future leaders.
- **Thrive through change**: Develop the resilience to not just survive, but thrive in a constantly shifting environment, positioning yourself, your team and your organization on the leading edge in your industry.
- **Foster organizational learning**: Cultivate a culture where diversity, creativity and learning thrive, where performance, engagement and motivation are high — and turnover is no longer a costly bottom-line factor.

Feminine-Inspired Leadership isn't just a book; it's an experience that aims to transform how you lead and build leadership capacity in others on the journey. It will unlock your full potential and guide you toward meaningful change — the kind of change today's business leaders are called to create in their teams, organizations and communities.

Why you need and want this book

This book is designed to be highly adaptable — its principles and practices can be applied to a wide range of contexts and situations. Whether you're leading a small team or a large organization, facing internal challenges or external pressures, you'll find relevant ideas and strategies to help you overcome obstacles and achieve your goals.

This practical book is not meant to offer prescriptive solutions but rather to empower you to take the ideas presented here and apply them to your unique situation. Experiment, iterate and adapt as needed to find what works best for you and your team.

Let's get started!

CHAPTER 1

Why We Need a Feminine Reimagining of Leadership

Leadership isn't just some fancy title or position — it's about *you*. It's how you show up every single day — for yourself, your team and your organization. It's about creating spaces where people feel genuinely valued, inspired and ready to give their best. At its core, leadership is all about connection. It starts with *you* being intentional — about your actions, your words and the energy you bring to every interaction.

Most of the strategies and lessons you will read about in this book are connected to a concept I call feminine-inspired leadership. I'll expound on that in this chapter but before you dive in let's start by clearing up a couple of assumptions (or misconceptions).

Feminine-inspired leadership isn't about gender.

Leadership has never been about gender. But let's be honest — it's been shaped by gendered expectations, including a lot of traditionally masculine qualities and attributes. This includes control, authority, and the relentless focus on performance, tasks and outcomes, which has left us with a leadership culture that often feels hollow.

Feminine-inspired leadership is an approach that leverages attributes that we usually associate with the feminine paradigm. It is about tapping into our intuition, focusing on collaboration, leveraging diversity, bringing people together to resolve challenges and so much more. It's a way of leading that we will be exploring throughout this book.

Feminine-inspired leadership is about choosing to lead through:

- Connection over control
- Collaboration over competition
- Community over individualism

And no, it's not soft or weak. It's smart and strategic. It's effective. And it's what teams and organizational leaders are desperately in need of from its leaders. Leaders like you!

The heart of feminine-inspired leadership

Feminine-inspired leadership is about connecting with people and inspiring everyone around you to step into their best selves. It's about infusing the feminine into your leadership. It's about leading with empathy, building trust and inspiring collective success.

Here are five guiding principles to consider as you incorporate feminine-inspired leadership into your own authentic style of leading people. These are foundational to all of the information that will be covered in this book.

- **Relational leadership**
  True leadership thrives on relationships. When you prioritize connection and build trust, you create an environment where people feel heard and valued. Your team will rise when they know their voices matter and their contributions are seen.

- **Empathy and emotional intelligence**
  Leadership isn't just about delivering results; it's about how you engage with the people achieving them. Your ability to navigate relationships with empathy and emotional intelligence will set the tone for your team's success.

- **Empowering growth**

Great leaders don't claim to have all the answers. They ask better questions, mentor their teams and create opportunities for growth. By creating a learning environment and empowering those around you, you unleash the potential for enhanced performance, innovation and unprecedented results.

- **Shared decision-making**

  When you create an environment that invites diverse perspectives and encourages participatory processes, your team feels a deeper sense of ownership in the outcomes. Together, you make better decisions, rooted in collective wisdom rather than individual opinion.

- **Authenticity and courage**

  The best leaders are those who lead from their values not their ego. They use their values to guide them, especially during change and transition. Authenticity requires courage, to challenge outdated norms, advocate for what's right and inspire others to do the same.

Here's the truth: the model of leadership that emphasizes control, competition and individual dominance just doesn't work anymore. Feminine-inspired leadership flips that script. It's relational. It's about 'power to' not 'power over,' and leveraging your greatest asset, your people, to create unprecedented results.

The power of connection over control

Traditional leadership that relied on authority and compliance to drive results is no longer working. This outdated approach is insufficient for resolving challenges, navigating complexity or finding solutions to the pressing issues of today's business environment.

If you are reading this book you are likely open-minded about and giving serious consideration to integrating the feminine into your leadership approach. You recognize that the connection with your stakeholders is the true currency of impactful leadership. When you create connection:

- **You create alignment.** Teams rally around shared goals because they see and believe in the vision, not because they're told to comply. This shared sense of purpose fosters commitment and unites efforts toward meaningful outcomes.
- **You build trust.** Leadership grounded in integrity, empathy and purpose cultivates loyalty and strengthens relationships. Trust becomes the foundation for collaboration and innovation.
- **You empower others.** Leadership is no longer a solo act but a shared effort. By empowering those around you, you amplify your collective impact, driving creativity, growth and resilience across the organization.

This approach to leadership doesn't just address today's complexities; it creates environments where teams thrive, ideas flourish, and challenges are met with ingenuity and unity. Through connection, you inspire deeper collaboration, mutual understanding and a sense of community. This is a leadership approach perfectly aligned with today's demands.

The best way to convince those who are hesitant — namely, those who are leading from a traditional approach — is to model the non-traditional feminine-inspired way of leading. You need to demonstrate the difference this makes in changing your organizational culture and the results that can be achieved when you know how to build a collaborative learning team.

And if you are at the helm of your organization you must intentionally choose leaders who lead from this approach and train the ones you currently have in this feminine-inspired leadership approach, thereby creating work cultures where people thrive and you position your organization at the cutting edge of your industry.

Embracing power for good

Power is neither good nor bad — it's how you use it that matters. Feminine-inspired leadership reframes power as a force for positive change. It's about shifting the focus from personal gain to collective good. From me to we to us.

Power, when wielded collaboratively, can unite people, drive growth and transform workplaces into environments where everyone thrives.

Leadership is not about being perfect; it's about being intentional. The best leaders:

- **Cultivate self-awareness.** They understand their values, their triggers and their impact on others.
- **Stay adaptive.** They embrace change and inspire their teams to navigate transitions with confidence.
- **Lead with empathy.** They prioritize understanding and responding to others' needs, creating a foundation for trust and collaboration.

Leading with a feminine-inspired approach requires courage. It means going about leadership in a different way, prioritizing connection over control; valuing collaboration over competition; and focusing on community over individualism.

Practise this feminine-inspired approach. It's leadership that values people as much as performance. It dares to explore possibilities instead of settling for the status quo.

You don't need to have all the answers to lead this way. What matters is your willingness to ask thoughtful questions, challenge old norms and invite others to co-create the future with you.

Transformative leadership has many dimensions

As we begin this leadership learning journey, let's reflect on the depth and dimensions of leadership explored throughout these pages. These are more than principles to adopt; they are calls to action, opportunities to rethink how you lead, inspire and leave an enduring impact.

- **Leadership and shared language.** Leadership begins with clarity, an understanding that transcends roles or titles. At its heart leadership is about amplifying collective voices, empowering others and guiding through challenges. It's a practice of creating environments where people feel seen, valued and encouraged to reach their highest potential.
- **Shared vision.** At the core of effective leadership is a unifying vision, a purpose that connects and energizes. When leaders craft a vision that aligns with the team's aspirations, it ignites commitment and fosters belonging. This shared vision acts as a guiding star, focusing efforts on what matters most. It is through alignment with this vision that we turn ideas into action and dreams into meaningful outcomes.
- **Planning.** Planning bridges the gap between where we are and where we aim to be. It's not just setting goals — it's creating a deliberate path forward. With clear milestones and aligned actions, progress becomes both intentional and inspiring.
- **Resource management and co-ordination.** Leadership is about making the most of resources — not just assets but the diversity, unique talents, creativity and passion of the people we lead. When

leaders invite people to fully engage, they transform potential into performance. Effective co-ordination ensures efforts are maximized, waste is minimized, and structures are in place so that teams are empowered to excel. It's about creating the workplace environment and conditions for individuals and organizations to thrive together.

- **Personal mastery and self-awareness.** Great leadership begins within. Personal mastery is the practice of self-awareness and growth, embracing our strengths, owning our vulnerabilities and leading with authenticity. When leaders commit to their own development, they inspire resilience and courage in others.

- **Organizational politics and stewardship.** Navigating organizational dynamics is a skill that needs to be honed. Stewardship challenges leaders to act in alignment with values, prioritizing the collective good over individual gain. It's about cultivating a culture of learning, building connections, and ensuring that leadership remains a service-oriented practice. True stewardship creates enduring value for organizations and the people they serve.

- **Risk-taking.** Courageous leadership embraces risk — not for its own sake but as a path to innovation and growth. Leaders who challenge outdated ways and methods create opportunities for transformation and progress. Transparent, ethical decision-making reflects integrity and ensures that bold actions serve the team and organization meaningfully.

These principles aren't soft — they're transformative. They make teams stronger, decisions better and cultures healthier.

Shaping your leadership legacy

Feminine-inspired leadership is about embracing the energy and qualities that bring caring, connectedness and understanding back into leadership. It's about creating environments where people flourish, not because of pressure but because of purpose.

At the end of the day, leadership isn't just about what you achieve; it's about the ripple effect you create. It's about showing up with courage, leading with empathy and igniting the passion in others to create the impossible together.

How you lead shapes everything — your team, your organization and even the environment around you.

Your leadership is the difference that can make a difference — in your team, your organization, your industry, your community and the world.

Make it count!

🔍 Reflection Questions

At the end of each chapter I'll provide reflection questions, here are a couple for you to set the tone.

1. **How am I showing up today in my leadership role?**

    What parts of the feminine-inspired leadership framework will you integrate into your leadership approach? How will you lead differently going forward?

    _____

    _____

    _____

    _____

2. **How do I currently demonstrate my trustworthiness in my daily leadership practice?**

    Think about how you show vulnerability, keep your promises and engage in honest dialogue. What evidence would your team point to that shows you are a trustworthy leader?

    _____

    _____

    _____

    _____

CHAPTER 2

Leading with Values That Fit — Personal, Team and Organizational

I worked with a vocational rehabilitation firm early in my professional career. As a consultant, they allowed me to work around my family commitments, to set my own hours, and independently manage my own time. As long as my client interviews, reports and vocational plans were submitted within the requisite timelines, my work schedule was my own. This was in the 1990s, long before working from home became commonplace. (I do remember friends saying that, given the opportunity to work in this manner, they would have spent their days on the couch watching sitcoms and snacking.)

Part of this work arrangement was billable hours so I had to have the discipline to structure my own work environment and track my hours in order to get paid. Obviously this environment is not for everyone, but for me and my partner — who worked shift work — it gave us the flexibility to work at times that were conducive to parenting our young children with minimal need for childcare outside the home. Having the ability to close the home office door and transition into the beehive of a busy family life to start dinner, to fold some laundry at lunch and to work later compiling reports when my daughters were asleep was a great way to achieve work-life harmony.

I valued family, independence and flexibility at this time in my career. Fortunately, these personal values aligned with my employer's organizational values and resulted in a 10-year term of employment. This example from my own career demonstrates how crucial it is for employers to define the values that underpin their organization and to ensure that they align with the values of their employees. This values alignment can ensure full engagement, extend tenure and generate a shared commitment about the way we work.

What are values?

Values are what you care about most as a leader, as a team, as an organization. Being able to clearly describe what that value looks like in practice is vitally important. For example, a tech startup would highly value thinking outside of the box (innovation), creativity and a high risk tolerance for all kinds of reasons whereas a human services organization would value individuals with compassion, service and commitment. Different organizations may share similar values but it's important to define, for example, what integrity or collaboration or innovation as values mean and look like in your organizational culture.

You can tell what an organization values by what leaders reward, either implicitly or explicitly, in the work environment and in what is encouraged or discouraged in the workplace. For example, if you value innovation you encourage trying new approaches and you are tolerant of risk-taking, which you view as learning not failure. You can also do the reverse. That is, you can observe behaviours that are endorsed through the organizational norms and determine what they value. The takeaway here is that both new and tenured staff are acutely aware of what the organization values by what the company rewards or condemns in their employees' behaviours.

For example, if a company values diversity of thought, you will see evidence of welcoming multiple perspectives, by norms that allow for individuals to contest the status quo and to share alternative perspectives in pursuit of the betterment of project outcomes, and being able to do so with no fear of reprisal. When this value is not present, those who share a perspective that is contrary to the organizational authority are marginalized or worse, set as an example for others about the consequences of vocalizing a perspective that is counter to the culture.

If the company values collaboration, which is a traditionally feminine trait, you will see that reflected in policies and practices that require cross-functional team conversations or structures that broaden stakeholder consultation. They would reward leaders who are best able to create collaborations and partnerships that obtain desired outcomes by providing those individuals with high-stakes initiatives, like keeping funders satisfied. Rewards might include promotions to highly coveted positions for leaders who are able to build collaboration (and the other organizational values) into all aspects of their work.

I cannot overemphasize how important it is to understand the essential role of values in shaping organizational identity and guiding leadership actions. Values are another time-honoured feminine-inspired practice that provide guidance for decision-making and assist people in choosing the 'right' course of action that aligns with the organization's mission and vision. Organizations that are lost or directionless usually have not taken the time to clarify their values, what those values look like in practice, the expectations about how those values are to be applied in the workplace and why they matter. Values are a lens to apply; they guide everything from strategic directives to making daily decisions to navigating in crisis. This is why your values-alignment check should include noticing whether your values skew to the masculine — or feminine-inspired. If you're trying to embrace feminine-inspired leadership in an organization that explicitly values masculine-inspired traits, you're never going to make it.

Alignment of values in the workplace is correlated with organizational health, so just like your personal health, taking time to carve out those values and practise them ensures wellness in the workplace. Whereas, if there is incongruency between stated values that are shared as part of employee onboarding and the values that are practised, that is a problem that leads to confusion, mistrust and has a negative impact on stakeholders, from frontline employees to partners outside of the organization. In simple terms, it's like giving mixed messages. We say we want this and that it's important to us, yet we reward behaviour that is the opposite. Taking time to define your organizational values will provide guidelines for everyone and clarity on how all employees are expected to work together.

As a leader, you can do a values alignment check at every stage of the employment life cycle. When recruiting and hiring, understanding your organization's values allows you to select employees who are a good fit for your culture. For example, if you and your organization value competitiveness versus collaboration, you will seek out employees who demonstrate that propensity and share your organizational value of competitiveness. This may be a necessary trait in an individual commission sales-based role. On the other hand, the ability to work collaboratively may be necessary if the job involves working as part of an integrated team, like the one I was on as a psychiatric occupational therapist, where multiple team members were all integral to gathering data to diagnose and treat our patients in a rehabilitation facility.

There are various approaches to convey your organizational values to new hires that go beyond listing them on your website, the wall in your reception area or your most recent community report. The best approach is to review them as part of the onboarding process. Spend time discussing the meaning of those values, the reason they were chosen and the way they are expected to be applied. And include examples of how they are expected to be demonstrated in employees' actions and team relations.

Another critical time that organizational values can assist is when you are in conflict or a crisis. In these situations, these values become your north star, your moral compass, guiding decisions, behaviours, interactions to help you to navigate through uncharted waters as a team or as an organization. Here is an example of a prompt that might elicit some reflection: In moments of conflict, uncertainty or crisis, which of your core values serve as your 'north star'? How have they helped you navigate difficult decisions or conversations?

Teaching the importance of values alignment

At Organizations by Design Inc., some of the most important work we engage in with our clients is time spent as a whole organization clearly identifying their values. Prior to their team learning session each person completes a values assessment. I use the **Personal Values Assessment** which can be completed online in under 10 minutes and generates a report for each team member. This becomes the foundation of a values conversation that evolves throughout the session. At the end, everyone is clear on both their personal and the organizational values, how to integrate them into their work and whether they are a 'fit' for the organization. One client said: "In my former role, I always felt like a square peg in a round hole and now I understand the reason!" Values encapsulate who you are as an organization and provide the framework for aligning actions with aspirations.

Aligned values foster a sense of belonging, purpose and commitment among employees. They are not just words on a page; they are the way we agree to work together and they create a roadmap for our behaviour and organizational excellence. They are one of the glues that bind us and allow us to work together, knowing our mutually agreed-upon ways of conducting ourselves on behalf of the organization.

Although values will differ from individual to individual, having most of your personal values align with your organizational values is essential for engagement and inclusion in the workplace. The list of values is long but there are work-specific values that include integrity, empowerment and teamwork. A comprehensive list of **Core Values in the Workplace** can be found in the resources section of this chapter. I find this list to be a helpful reference when working with teams to determine which values are shared amongst individuals. More convergence around similar values is directly proportional with engagement and a sense of belonging.

Exploring core values

Core values are those that consistently emerge in organizational cultures that prioritize learning and they include: integrity, honesty, openness, transparency, stewardship, responsibility and accountability. Honesty and transparency are not just buzzwords but are essential for cultivating trust in leadership and amongst the team. They are the cornerstone of the feminine-inspired leadership approach which roots action in personal and collective values to drive meaningful, sustainable impact.

Knowing this and being able to foster trust and set up your team environment for learning is one thing. Being able to put this into practice successfully as a leader is another, and is more challenging. I explore this more in the chapters on trust, thinking and learning. There, I will examine how embracing these values of integrity, honesty, openness, transparency, stewardship, responsibility and accountability leads to open dialogue, innovation and a culture of learning. In fact throughout the book I will continue to reinforce that integrity is the cornerstone of good leadership and trust. By integrity, I mean being your authentic self in every situation, practising your leadership values, and ensuring that there is alignment between your leadership values and how you show up every day and in every situation.

Embracing stewardship and accountability

I have found a recent shift in working with clients. Leaders often struggle with the balance between the individual employee or stakeholder needs and the organizational needs. Regardless of which generational demographic you belong to, it is important to remember, and remind employees, that they are compensated to provide service and stewardship to clients, and that they have responsibility and accountability in their particular organizational role. Simply put, your employer pays you to do your role in service to the organizational mission and vision. Your job is to do that well.

In turn, the employer has a responsibility to create an environment that embraces their stated values and empowers individuals to apply them, thereby contributing to the collective success. The key here is ensuring that there are clearly defined examples of what those values look like in practice. This is another exercise well worth spending time doing. It involves generating real-time examples of desirable behaviours. Members of the leadership team should be modelling those values in action in each of their interactions with stakeholders daily. This is about walking the talk.

Organizational values are truly the foundation of your organization. Without clearly defining them, having specific examples of what they look like in practice and holding everyone accountable, you are like a rudderless ship at sea going in whatever direction the storm of the day is taking you. In that situation, your employees are at a loss as to how to behave and conduct their work. If you have not taken the time to establish and articulate your values — not just on a wall or in your annual report but through a robust team engagement session — you should. I promise it will be time well spent.

🔍 Reflection Questions

1. **Which of my personal values do I see most clearly reflected in my current leadership style?**

   How do these values influence the way you lead your team or organization?

   _____

   _____

   _____

   _____

   _____

2. **When was the last time I experienced a sense of values alignment or misalignment at work?**

   What impact did that have on your motivation, performance, or relationships?

   _____

   _____

   _____

   _____

   _____

3. **How do our organizational values show up in daily practice — in policies, decision-making and how success is recognized or rewarded?**

   Where do you see strengths and where might there be gaps?

   _____
   _____
   _____
   _____
   _____

4. **In moments of conflict, uncertainty or crisis, which of my core values serve as my 'north star'?**

   How have they helped you navigate difficult decisions or conversations?

   _____
   _____
   _____
   _____
   _____

5. **What conversations or actions could I initiate to ensure better alignment between my team's behaviours and my organization's stated values?**

    Who needs to be involved and what would be the first step?

    _____

    _____

    _____

    _____

    _____

CHAPTER 3

Trust Is Your Leadership Currency

In this chapter we will explore the role trust plays in facilitating difficult conversations, embracing diverse perspectives and creating psychologically safe environments.

Building trust in relationships and healthy teams is essential for fostering collaboration, improving communication and achieving success. It develops cohesion, resilience and innovation within teams, organizations and communities. Some of the key behaviours that provide evidence of trust are described below.

When team members demonstrate their ability to perform tasks, solve problems and meet expectations.

In a team, knowing that each person has the required skills and expertise to contribute effectively to the group builds confidence and trust in one another's areas of competence. One of the exercises that works really well when working with teams is to have them showcase the unique skill sets they bring to the team via a **Skills Inventory,** which is documented and accessible across the team. This would be a living document so everyone is aware of who the go-to people are, allowing them to tap into these assets. A more specific example is when I am working with teams on a certain topic — say change endurance — we do an assessment on change readiness. After individually completing the exercise, team members are invited to share their strengths, resulting in an inventory of change-readiness skills.

Reliability is trusting that others will follow through on their commitments. It is another means to gauge and build trust. In a team setting this involves meeting deadlines, being consistent and delivering what was promised. Team members rely on each other to perform their responsibilities and support one another. When people do what they say that builds trust — they know they can count on each other.

Integrity involves acting with honesty and aligning actions with values. When team members demonstrate that they will do what's right, even when it's difficult, this establishes trust. Integrity is key to long-term relationships and creating an atmosphere of mutual respect and accountability.

Vulnerability contributes to building trust. It is about being open, sharing weaknesses and admitting mistakes. This type of trust creates psychological safety, where team members feel comfortable expressing themselves without fear of judgment. It's essential for creativity, learning and team cohesion.

Another measure involves trusting in the good intentions and motivations of others. Team members who believe that others are working toward the same common goals and have the team's best interests in mind are more likely to collaborate effectively. Intentional trust is grounded in the assumption that actions are driven by a desire to contribute positively.

Emotional trust is built when people feel understood and supported emotionally. In a team, this trust involves empathy, active listening and caring for one another's well-being. When team members feel that others truly care about them on an emotional level, it strengthens bonds and increases engagement.

Being able to share information openly, truthfully and without fear of misinterpretation or dishonesty is another important component of trust. When team members feel confident that the information they receive is accurate and transparent, it fosters stronger decision-making and problem-solving.

By nurturing these different types of trust, teams can create a foundation for strong, healthy relationships that promote collaboration, transparency and high performance. As leaders, we are responsible for creating cultures of openness, authenticity and mutual respect. And we must model trust if we are to build it within our teams.

Let's dive into three strategies that will enhance your trust-building capacity by leaps and bounds. Difficult conversations. Leveraging diversity. And creating psychologically safe workspaces.

Difficult conversations

Difficult conversations are inevitable in interpersonal and organizational dynamics. They require courage, empathy, skilful communication and a process that we will walk through together in this book. Having the skills to manage these conversations well can positively impact the level of trust in one-on-one, team and organizational relationships.

A client reached out to us after reading one of our *Feminine-Inspired Leadership Insights* weekly blogs that focused on creating confidence in communication for leaders. They invited us to spend a day with their leadership team, providing them with both the tools and the confidence to have difficult conversations.

This group was made up of mostly social workers and psychologists, who are great at having these conversations with their clients. But there was much angst about having difficult conversations with one another, their peers and their direct reports. After the day-long workshop, in our closing circle one of the psychologists said: "We learn about how to be great psychologists but (they) never taught us 'how to' be leaders, and in our formal training they certainly did not show us how to have these conversations with each other in a professional environment. We need more of this type of practical training in our roles as leaders."

So to ensure that your next difficult conversation goes really well, let's review the steps, strategies and structure that set the stage for a successful conversation. It's imperative to create a safe, supportive environment and to set a positive tone for the conversation, where the employee feels safe to discuss challenges and is open to feedback.

1. **I suggest you begin with a mindset shift.** At the start of any difficult conversation, I want to emphasize the importance of shifting the focus from fault-finding to identifying growth opportunities. The goal is to support your team member's development and strengthen the relationship between the two of you. One proven way to do this is to include reflection or coaching questions in your one-on-one sessions that have them explore what they might do differently in the future or what they learned about themselves. This coaching approach encourages them to be quintessential learners.

2. **Prepare for the conversation by gathering facts to ensure you have all the relevant data and concrete factual observations.** This evidence should be objective and focused on behaviours, rather than personal attributes. Next, identify the desired outcome by clarifying what you hope to achieve from the conversation. Is it to improve specific skills, adjust behaviour or set new goals? Lastly, do a temperature check on yourself — are you emotionally neutral going into the conversation? Having a

conversation while emotionally charged can be damaging to the relationship and the outcome, so do that emotional check-in to get grounded and focused before this type of conversation.

3. **Begin the conversation with why the meeting is taking place and provide context.** In many cases you will find it helpful to approach this step when scheduling the meeting with the employee so they don't feel surprised or ambushed going into it. Then, clearly state the specific area where they are not meeting expectations or the identified area of concern. Use factual, non-emotional language, and focus on observable behaviours. Example: "I've noticed that deadlines have been missed on several recent projects, which affects the overall team's progress."

4. **Next, shift the conversation to a growth mindset by asking questions that encourage the employee to reflect on their performance and identify areas for improvement.** Example: "What do you think are the challenges you're facing in meeting these deadlines?" Then, work together to develop a plan of action. This could include additional training, adjusting workloads or setting clear expectations. Example: "Let's explore ways to manage your workload more effectively. What support do you need to meet these deadlines?" Agree on goals and ensure they understand what success looks like in clearly defined behaviours and/or expected outcomes — and by when.

5. **Express your commitment to helping the employee succeed.** Offer resources, mentorship or regular feedback to support their development. Example: "I'm here to support you in this process. Let's work together to make sure you have what you need to succeed." Prior to ending the meeting, summarize the key points discussed and confirm that the employee understands the expectations and the support available to them. Lastly, reinforce

your confidence in their ability to improve and express your optimism about their future contributions.

Given a choice, the majority of us would prefer to avoid having difficult conversations. But addressing concerns, conflicts, misunderstandings and differing perspectives is essential to building trust and aligning individual behaviour with organizational norms. As a leader you can transform individuals and teams by approaching difficult conversations with openness, curiosity, a commitment to understanding and clarity of expectations.

Leveraging diverse perspectives

Another key area that can build trust is being able to embrace and integrate diverse perspectives amongst team members. If you only choose team members whose thoughts and beliefs align with your own, you're left with no one to challenge your ideas, leaving you without critical feedback. As a leader, creating a team culture that values every individual's unique experiences, backgrounds and viewpoints builds trust and belonging. But how do you do that, you might be asking, without spending countless hours or days hearing everyone out?

The easiest way is to state it clearly and then demonstrate it every day. Make it your practice to seek out other team or peers' perspectives, to listen to their viewpoints. Tap into those individuals who are identified experts or have experience in dealing with a similar issue they may have encountered. When diverse perspectives are recognized, teams can approach challenges from multiple angles, enhancing creativity and fostering resilience.

But the real secret is framing the questions. If they are too open-ended you will spend days hearing people out, which can become time-consuming to a fault. But if you craft questions that seek to collect input about a particular aspect that is within their purview, then you will be mining gold. Here's an example: As a senior executive, you may have a policy that needs to be implemented and that is crafted on industry best practice. Running it by the staff who will be responsible for implementing the policy in your organization and allowing them to provide input about implementation will allow you to make subtle tweaks that will allow for near-seamless integration.

Another great tool is the **IAP2** (International Association for Public Participation) developed for public consultations. It can easily be implemented to assist you in clarifying the level of engagement, which is critical. You will see that this tool runs the spectrum from for-information-only to there-are-no-parameters. I like to describe this as identifying the 'sandbox' that people are invited to play in. You must clearly outline that which is outside the sandbox or non-negotiable, like regulations that you must comply with or decisions that have been made. Then offer potential solutions that address the issue framed by the question, within the sandbox. By doing this, you invite your team to share their inputs and diverse perspectives with a clear question and parameters that define the input they have in that particular situation.

I think it goes without saying but I'll say it anyway. It's imperative that you tap into that vast diversity and leverage it to its full extent. The ability to do this taps into the full potential of your team and can be a competitive advantage and very satisfying to your team. Doing this will show that you value, respect and trust your team. It also helps you become that innovative, creative, cutting-edge, unstoppable team.

Creating psychological safety

For me, psychological safety refers to an environment where individuals feel comfortable taking risks and expressing ideas without fear of judgment or reprisal, where there is mutual respect for others and the team, and organizational norms are followed. There is a lot packed into that statement. So let's unpack it.

Establishing an environment where people feel comfortable taking risks and expressing ideas is done through establishing rules of engagement or shared commitments. Taking risks and expressing ideas is just half of this equation. Doing it without fear, or judgment or reprisal is the other part that some leaders fail to adhere to, resulting in a collapse in trust.

How we receive those who take risks or share ideas will determine whether people will stop or continue to share them. People notice if you are receptive to or dismissive of hearing ideas, whether you create structures to seek them out and whether and how they are used. They also pay particular attention to what happens when someone challenges a perspective, or takes a risk or shares a new idea.

So what about the part of the definition of psychological safety that addresses doing this in a mutually respectful manner? This is where the leader sets the tone and expectations about how we share — and what is acceptable and unacceptable in our interactions with one another. A leader does this both by role-modelling respectful behaviour and by calling out disrespectful behaviour. That is, teaching what mutual respect looks like amongst the team members or with peers. Remember the old adage: We can agree to disagree and still do that in a respectful manner. And as a team, we have to establish ways that we engage together at times when we are having difficult conversations and during times when we are expressing amazing possibilities. Being able to do this builds a bond of trust between team members.

The last part of the definition looks at doing this within the team and organizational norms. Norms are simply agreed-upon ways in which we work together. They are unique to each team and each organization. The more explicit we can make the norms as leaders, the easier it is for people to understand and abide by them. For example, in one organization it may be the norm to be constantly challenging the status quo as a means of staying on the cutting edge to ensure constant innovation. In another organization, there could be a norm to be extremely cautious about making even small changes to ensure that risk management remains the utmost in importance.

However, where this really comes into play is when we watch and see what happens when someone draws attention to a norm that is being contravened. In some organizational cultures you will be a celebrated role model and in others, with very different norms, that would result in termination of your employment, with or without cause. In a workplace where feminine-inspired leadership is the norm, leaders are open-minded about hearing from employees about organizational issues.

How you handle risk-takers and people's ideas says a lot and will signal to people whether it is safe to continue to do this. I hope in your situation that how you set up your team environment, demonstrate and respond in all situations results in a psychologically safe environment because that will allow you to create a milieu where incredible things happen within and through your team!

Trust is the cornerstone of collaboration, helping teams navigate challenges, build relationships and achieve shared goals. Leaders can nurture trust by embracing difficult conversations, leveraging diversity and creating psychologically safe environments. A culture of trust fosters creativity, innovation and sustainable success within teams and organizations, so it is well worth the effort.

🔍 Reflection Questions

1. **How do I currently demonstrate trust in my daily leadership practice?**

    Think about how you show vulnerability, keep your promises and engage in honest dialogue. What evidence would your team point to that shows you are a trustworthy leader?

    _____

    _____

    _____

    _____

2. **When was the last time I had a difficult conversation that built (or damaged) trust?**

    What mindset, language or behaviours did I bring into that conversation? If I could do it over again, what would I do differently to create a more psychologically safe outcome?

    _____

    _____

    _____

    _____

3. **Do my team members feel safe speaking up, offering dissenting views or taking risks?**

   What have I seen, heard or experienced that would affirm (or challenge) this belief? What actions have I taken to invite diverse perspectives into our decision-making processes?

   _____

   _____

   _____

   _____

   _____

4. **How do I respond when a team member fails, makes a mistake or challenges a norm?**

   Is my reaction reinforcing or eroding trust? How can I better use these moments to build psychological safety, model integrity and create learning opportunities?

   _____

   _____

   _____

   _____

   _____

5. **What small, consistent behaviours could I adopt to deepen trust across my team?**

   Consider actions like active listening, checking in regularly, publicly recognizing contributions or asking for feedback. Which one to two micro-actions could I commit to starting this week?

   _____

   _____

   _____

   _____

   _____

CHAPTER 4

Communication That Connects — Even When It's Tough

Communication is how we inspire teams, provide clarity, navigate complex situations, champion change and navigate difficult but necessary conversations. It is imperative to constantly be honing our communication skills as leaders and team members, and reminding ourselves often that communication is not merely about conveying information — it's about forging meaningful connections, fostering understanding and navigating the complexities of human interaction.

Communication can be transformative in itself and is a must for supporting every aspect of change. Rather than dwelling on the technical aspects of communication, in this chapter I present some feminine-inspired nuances of communication.

A client story

We embarked on a learning journey with a client, a not-for-profit organization that offers residential programs for children who have been sexually abused. Our aim was to develop their leadership team's skills to express themselves confidently and build their ability to communicate assertively, especially during tough conversations.

Going into the training, members of this leadership team highlighted challenges related to leadership transitions, lack of clarity in vision and difficulty in managing change when one lacks either the confidence or the skills to communicate effectively. Most reported experiencing obstacles such as feeling overwhelmed by responsibilities, struggling with team dynamics, and not having the necessary leadership and communication skills to advance the work of their teams. Many wanted to build stronger connections with their teams, enhance their decision-making abilities and foster more effective collaboration. All of these require advanced communication skills.

Many of them envisioned a future where they could confidently lead their teams, create meaningful impact and feel fulfilled in their leadership roles. They described wanting to create a leadership environment where they are respected, empowered and able to make a positive difference in their organization. They also wanted to better understand the role that communication played in making that vision a reality.

In our closing circle at the end of our day of training and in their written evaluations, this leadership team highlighted the value of learning practical communication skills, acquiring tools and frameworks and the opportunity to practise them as part of their learning experience. They also valued the exploration of deeper, underlying issues that were influencing their communication challenges, particularly when they had an opportunity in our leadership development session to shift their perspective and address root causes or obstacles. They appreciated and expressed a preference for our interactive facilitated approach that offered real-time feedback, where they got to do role plays and get feedback from their peers, allowing them to apply new learning directly to their work situations. This approach is what makes feminine-inspired leadership different.

Communication exchanges

We have all experienced a communication exchange that has gone sideways. Perhaps it was because of the words, the way the communication exchange was delivered or the way the communication was received or perceived by the listener.

With clients, we often discuss that it is truly amazing how different people observing the same situation have such different interpretations and perspectives. This is an important lesson to remember as a leader. Your communication to your team may be perceived differently by each member of your team, especially if you are a new leader and they have no previous experience with you and your communication style.

As a young leader, I participated in a *Leadership Edmonton* cohort and learned from a wise fellow participant about how as individuals we view the world through our life and world experiences. Our perceptions and perspectives are lenses or filters through which we see the world. Because each of us has had completely different life experiences, we see and interpret each communication exchange – whether it is a corporate memo or town hall address from the CEO or a fellow colleague's contributions in a team meeting — through our own lens. A simple example to highlight this might be a team leader who says to a direct report: "I noticed the last three reports you sent in missed the submission deadline." Some people perceive this as negative feedback or a reprimand, while others may interpret it as an observation of behaviour and others might construe that this is the beginning of a performance management conversation.

So how we view every communication through our life lens has a significant impact on our experience, understanding and perception of what we are hearing. As leaders we need to communicate to ensure understanding, clarity and connection. As leaders we also need to check out that the intended message was received. The importance of establishing shared understanding is an ongoing process that we commit to as leaders, one that with practice results in fewer misunderstandings and misinterpretations.

The power of shared commitments

As a leader, developing shared commitments is a crucial element of a good communicator. Shared commitments are the act of committing time as a team to engage in a conversation about how you agree you are going to work together.

At the start of every client engagement session and with every team that I have led, I allocate time to create our shared commitments. This process is referred to in many different ways. Rules of engagement, boundaries of action or a team charter. You can use whatever term resonates, but the important point is to ensure you do this. It makes a tremendous difference in the team's working relationship.

Shared commitments are the contract or agreement that sets the parameters for how we commit to learning together or working together as a team. I cannot overstate the impact of taking time to do this and the power it has to create an environment for doing amazing work together. We do this every time we start one of our leadership learning programs. Participants are invited to generate a list of what they need to create a safe learning space, such as eliminating all distractions and focusing on the discussion, ensuring respectful dialogue even if there are differing perspectives, being able to seek clarification, etc. Here is an actual example of the shared commitments generated by our last *Building Confidence in Communication for Leaders* cohort:

Shared Commitments

1. **No exterior distractions:** e.g. turn off cellphones and other devices to be fully present and engaged.
2. **Confidentiality:** What happens in the group stays in the group to allow open sharing. Also, what happens outside of the group comes back into the group.
3. **Permission:** Give yourself permission to be vulnerable, understanding and respectful. Learning involves being open to challenge - and stretching.
4. **Engage:** Participants have permission to share their thoughts, ideas and insights.
5. **Inquire:** Seeking clarification and asking curious questions is part of learning — there can be no judgment.
6. **Engage authentically:** Appreciate we are all at different places as leaders and learners.
7. **Equity of voice:** Be mindful of the amount of time spent talking and listening, and the amount of time as an individual you have the floor.

Setting shared commitments at the start of an online workshop allows me as a facilitator to create a space that builds a safe learning environment for people from different organizations, who have never met to do some intensive sharing and learning. This has the same impact in terms of setting the tone at the start of all our feminine-inspired leadership learning experiences (programs) with our clients. I know from experience with my own teams and clients that when you take your team through this exercise, the impact it can have is profound because it sets the tone for having deep conversations.

This should be a non-negotiable exercise if you are embracing a feminine-inspired leadership approach. It will allow you to identify the way you want to work and the amazing things you can achieve together. The caveat is that you must be committed to holding one another to these ways of being together that you have established. This is not a one-time experience. You must revisit these shared commitments regularly (e.g. quarterly or annually) and each time a new team member joins the team. It allows you to orient new members to the team culture, and periodic review allows time to determine whether these shared commitments are still relevant and being practised as a team.

In this chapter's resource section there is a link to some examples of these agreements and a process to set your team up for success. Remember it's not about adopting a pre-existing set, but about having a conversation and creating your own shared commitments, rules of engagement or team charter. It's not important what you call them, but that they are meaningful and reflect how you want to show up, behave and work as a team.

Navigating filters and perspectives

Building on the previous section, understanding the diverse filters and lenses through which people perceive the world and how each individual's personal experiences, worldview and cultural backgrounds shape communication and interpretation is a critical foundation for communicating effectively as a leader.

If you have not yet been introduced to the ladder of inference, a cognitive and critical thinking tool, then you need to add it to your leadership toolkit to prevent yourself from jumping to premature conclusions. This tool improves quick decision-making, results in better communication and enhances self-awareness.

You can use it in many leadership situations, including times where communication has gone astray. It provides a simple model to help us understand how the observations, data, beliefs, meanings, assumptions, conclusions and actions individuals take are impacted by the information they see, hear or infer.

We will talk about the ladder of inference more in the chapter on thinking. It will expand your understanding about the importance of communication, and more importantly, it will remind you to check out how your message is being heard — sometimes in ways you might not have imagined.

Power of perspective and shared language

So, given we each have our own unique perspectives that come from our life experiences, and we each hear things through our filters, it is important to understand different perspectives and create shared language as leaders. Engaging in these practices ensures shared understanding, provides clarity and reduces misunderstandings.

I have a coaching client, let's refer to her as Cindy. In one of our sessions, she talked about how members of the team did not demonstrate the same urgency that she felt in terms of completion of client orders, explaining that they worked at the same pace on all jobs, and that in her absence from the workplace, they were unable to adjust their work priority and reallocate resources to get an order done by the deadline, resulting in higher rush shipping costs. When we looked at this, she was able to see that her commitment to getting the work done was not shared amongst her team, nor did they have a shared definition of 'rush order.' Once she was able to provide clarity, expected behaviours and related practices, there was a clear understanding amongst the team members about how to respond when a rush order came into the shop.

Shared language, defining what we mean when we use a specific term, is something that we do when we are introducing new concepts or tools in our leadership development programs. However, it is equally applicable when you are introducing a new concept in your industry to your team, to ensure that everyone is operating from the same definition. So when we say this, we mean this, and this is what that looks like or how we use it in our work.

Even when a team like Cindy's has shared language, there are often differing interpretations that require checking out through questions to ensure understanding and ultimately unity on the team to move toward the same goal or outcome.

The art of active listening

Active listening is the distinction between hearing words and truly understanding underlying emotions and meanings being conveyed. My definition of active listening involves fully concentrating, understanding and repeating back what the other person says.

Techniques such as reflecting back what you've heard, asking open-ended questions, and being mindful of non-verbal cues demonstrate active listening. And being fully present in conversations — free from distractions — shows that the person speaking is your top priority in that moment.

Active listening is vital for resolving conflicts and fostering a supportive environment where team members feel heard. There is an active listening checklist and guiding questions that I provide to my clients as a reference for practising the art of active listening. It has been built over time from various sources and my own practical experiences having these types of conversations. You'll find a great article on **Active Listening** in the resources section for this chapter.

The courage to have difficult conversations

I know for some of you, you have a strong desire to avoid difficult conversations – and by that, I mean things that need to be addressed that might be uncomfortable or the conflict you fear may arise from the discussion. But avoidance will not serve you well. Looking at this from a different perspective, you will see these conversations as an opportunity for growth and transformation for yourself, as well as within your team or organization. And they rarely go as badly as you think they might.

Other benefits of having difficult conversations include:

- **Resolving issues:** Addressing problems in a timely, objective and intentional manner prevents them from festering and causing bigger issues later.
- **Improving relationships:** Open communication builds trust and respect with colleagues.
- **Building a healthy work environment:** This fosters a culture where concerns can be raised constructively and issues can be explored in a manner that facilitates learning.

Let's face it, these conversations can be stressful. But by approaching them strategically, we can turn them into productive experiences that benefit both ourselves, those who report to us and our work environment.

Handling difficult conversations well provides ample opportunities for individual, team and organizational learning to occur. We will dive deeper into that in our chapter on learning. For now, let's focus on the basics of how to have these learning conversations and the importance of setting them up as opportunities to grow using this framework:

Pre-conversation preparation

- **Centre yourself:** Take deep breaths and practise mindfulness to maintain composure.
- **Define the problem:** Clearly identify the issue you want to address.
- **Consider their perspective:** What might their concerns be? How do they see the situation?
- **Plan talking points:** Outline key points you want to communicate, but avoid scripting everything.

During the conversation, use these communication techniques:

- **Active listening:** Give them your full attention and show you're trying to understand. Summarize to confirm understanding.
- **Focus on facts:** Frame your points with specific examples and data, not accusations. Instead of "you're always missing deadlines," say "the last two projects were delivered a day late."
- **Maintain respect:** Use a calm and professional tone, avoid personal attacks.

Finding solutions for collaborative problem-solving:

- **Identify common ground:** Look for areas where your perspectives overlap.
- **Brainstorm solutions together:** Work collaboratively to find solutions that address both sides' concerns.
- **Set action items:** Decide on clear next steps with defined ownership and deadlines.

Individual communication and personality styles

In addition to the language, terminology and tone we use to convey our messages to and from one another, it's important to view language as a tool for unity and understanding, promoting collaboration and increasing understanding.

Tools like communication or personality self-assessments can assist us to better understand individual communication preferences and the varied personalities of the members of our team. Although there are many of these types of assessments available for free online, two of my favourites are: 4 Communications Styles and the 16 Personalities Test.

In the **4 Communications Style Self-Assessment** we look to identify the individual's primary communication style and to develop a more assertive style, which is important for effective communication, especially when we are having crucial conversations.

The **16 Personalities** is a free personality assessment, based on the Myers Briggs Type Indicator. As someone who has been trained to administer and interpret theMyers Briggs, it's my recommendation that you use a certified consultant to be able to interpret and debrief the results of these online tools. And wherever possible, use the Myers Briggs, which has higher reliability and validity than knock-off assessments. Even with the Myers Briggs, the self-assessed and reported types are often off by a letter or two. This could result in a personality finding that is not reflective of the individual's communication style.

I really enjoy using these types of assessments as a leader, as a consultant and as a facilitator in our programs. These tools help us understand each other, allow us to see and leverage the strengths in our differences and identify other's preferences. And they are fun, if used ethically and for the right reasons.

Although my performance appraisals were glowing over the years, I confess that there was a consistent commentary about my direct assertive communication style. And that, in combination with my personality style, often resulted in feedback that my communication needed to be tempered. I know now that some of that was related to the double-bind paradox where bold, confident, direct female leaders are perceived differently than male leaders who demonstrate these same characteristics. And that often, it was more about the receiver. Nonetheless, learning to adjust my communication style, to the receiver, has served me well.

As leaders, we need to ensure that we communicate with our team members in a manner that is meaningful to them. It's easiest for me to communicate with those who share my communication style and preferences, but I have finally internalized the lesson about adapting my style to others' preferences, while still conveying the message I want to communicate.

Balancing advocacy and inquiry

As a leader, your ability to communicate effectively depends on finding the right balance between advocacy and inquiry. Advocacy is about clearly expressing views and your ideas, sharing your perspective and making recommendations. Inquiry, on the other hand, is about seeking others' perspective, which involves asking questions, actively listening and being genuinely curious about what others think.

When you balance these two approaches, you create space for open and meaningful dialogue and good thinking. For example, instead of dominating a meeting with your views, you might share your thoughts and then invite others to weigh in. This approach encourages better decisions by bringing in diverse perspectives.

A balanced dialogue doesn't just happen — it requires you to practise humility, curiosity and respect. It's about creating an environment where people feel safe to share their ideas, even if those ideas challenge the status quo. When team members know their input is valued, they are more likely to contribute, which strengthens trust, innovation and teamwork.

The **Artist Palette** visually illustrates the balance between advocacy and inquiry, emphasizing the importance of combining both for effective dialogue and decision-making. Fostering this balance isn't always easy, but it's worth the effort. By combining advocacy and inquiry, you can lead conversations that are both productive and empowering.

A few lessons to share

If you have worked with excellent communicators or poor ones, you know the value provided when someone integrates all these communication tools into their leadership approach, and the frustration, misunderstandings, complications and lost time that result from poor communicators.

Here are a few lessons I've learned about communication that I'll pass along so that you can benefit from them:

1. In the absence of communication, people will make stuff up, with rumours and gossip as a result. So whenever you can, communicate what is going on and the rationale.
2. Just like that telephone communication game we played as kids, remember that the message gets changed as it's passed along. Take time to ensure the message is checked at different points and there is clarity about the original message.
3. Use multiple methods of communication, especially for important messages, so that you ensure that those who process better with verbal, written or visual communications hear the message.

4. Put important things in writing, and ask a trusted peer to review it to ensure the intended message is being conveyed.
5. The rule that says it takes seven different times to get a message across is real. You will have to say it more than once, in many forums, repeated to ensure that it is heard, understood and being acted upon.
6. Time taken to ensure the intent and the expectations of a message is time well spent. Check by asking clarifying questions.
7. Be clear about what communication can be shared with whom and when, particularly if there are some confidentiality or timing issues.
8. Take the time to connect the dots for each individual, so that they understand the impact the message has for them or the work.
9. Have the courage to have difficult conversations. Everyone will grow from the experience.

Great communication isn't just a skill — it's a commitment. It requires you to step into difficult conversations with courage, listen with empathy, and articulate a vision that unites and empowers. Communication is the thread that ties together your values, intentions and actions, ultimately defining the culture and impact of your leadership. Keep this in mind: every interaction you have is an opportunity to shape understanding, inspire change and strengthen your team.

🔍 Reflection Questions

1. **Where in my leadership have I avoided a crucial conversation, and what was the cost — to me, to the other person and to the team culture?**

   What would it look like to revisit that conversation now with clarity, curiosity, and courage?

   _____

   _____

   _____

   _____

   _____

2. **How might my personal filters, lived experiences and communication preferences be shaping (or distorting) the way I interpret others — and the way I'm being interpreted?**

   How can I become more intentional in checking my assumptions?

   _____

   _____

   _____

   _____

3. **In what ways have I (unintentionally) contributed to misunderstandings, misalignment or disengagement through my communication — and what might I do differently next time?**

   How often do I truly check for shared understanding?

   _____
   _____
   _____
   _____
   _____

4. **How well do I balance advocacy (sharing my views) and inquiry (seeking others' perspectives)?**

   What would shift in my team dynamics if I practised deeper inquiry — especially in moments of tension or disagreement?

   _____
   _____
   _____
   _____
   _____

5. **Do my communication practices create safety, equity and space for all voices on my team — particularly those that are quieter, marginalized or different from mine?**

   What shared commitments or rules of engagement might we need to revisit or co-create to strengthen this?

   _____
   _____
   _____
   _____
   _____

CHAPTER 5

Learning Together — Growing Into Teams That Thrive

Learning is the difference that makes the difference. I learned this crucial lesson from a member of my service league who sat in an advisory capacity on our board of directors where I served as chair during my presidency.

After each board meeting we would meet to debrief and she would provide me with feedback on how she felt the meeting went and some commentary on my role as board chair. After one particular meeting, where another member of the board had shared a very strong opinion that was opposite to mine, we unpacked what had taken place. She shared an alternative perspective, that others on the board were not challenging my position, but actually helping me to see a different viewpoint that was outside my frame of reference. That day there was a significant shift in my thinking. I now viewed feedback and alternative viewpoints as a way for me to revisit my perspectives, to expand my understanding, to learn and to grow exponentially as a leader.

I'm drawing from decades of experience when I highlight the significance of creating an organizational learning culture as a cornerstone of effective leadership in today's complex business environment. I'll delve into the multifaceted aspects of learning and its pivotal role in nurturing a culture of growth, adaptability and innovation within your team and your organization.

This chapter highlights various dimensions of learning, from individual self-reflection to organizational evaluation. I aim to provide actionable insights and strategies for you to cultivate a dynamic and thriving learning organization.

A shared definition

Before diving deeper into the dimensions of fostering a learning culture, it's important to establish a shared understanding of what learning entails. Learning goes beyond acquiring knowledge or skills; it is a continuous process of exploration, adaptation and growth. In order to be able to do this, you must cultivate what Stanford educational psychologist Dr. Carol Dweck called a "growth mindset." You have to believe that people's skills and intelligence are not fixed qualities, as do your managers and your staff.

Learning is not confined to reading books or attending training sessions. It encompasses both formal education and experiential learning, shaping our perspectives, behaviours and capabilities over time. And most importantly, it's about intentionally implementing all these lessons as we move forward in our workspaces.

Why is this important? So that you can build on your learning the next time and can continuously improve your systems and most importantly, your outcomes. And you shouldn't do that in silos within the organization. You need to set up structures, such as team world cafe days, online interactive whiteboard and video recording, so that you can share lessons learned across your organization. You should do this as individuals, as teams and as an organization. You and your team must be committed to sharing what you have learned from your attempts and your trials. If you can do this, you will become a learning organization in the process.

I was intrigued by this concept of 'the learning organization' coined by Dr. Peter Senge in his book, ***The Fifth Discipline: The Art & Practice of the Learning Organization***. This was another great resource, introduced to me in my graduate studies, that resonated with my leadership approach. And I was privileged to study with Senge himself in Boston pre-pandemic. That intensive session filled in the gaps in my tattered copy of his book and deepened my education about team learning and learning organizations.

After Boston, my desire to share his brilliant concepts and to make his teachings accessible to my clients intensified. As such, the concept of a learning organization augments the feminine-inspired leadership approach. I have figured out how to integrate his theory into practice.

Learning cycle: adapting & relearning

In today's business landscape, the ability to adapt and relearn is paramount to individual and organizational success. I want to highlight the significance of embracing a learning cycle that involves continuous adaptation, experimentation, refinement and intentionally building structures for shared learning, so we can learn from our lessons.

Creating a conducive learning environment is pivotal to nurturing curiosity, innovation and collaboration within our organizations. It's important to foster a culture where learning is celebrated and individuals feel empowered to explore new ideas and share diverse perspectives. And this culture must be built on a foundation of trust and psychological safety, which is addressed in the chapter on trust. In cultures where this is not the case, team members are incentivized to hide their mistakes, overemphasize positive results and delay asking for help or input.

It bears repeating that a learning environment is not solely defined by formal training programs or resources. It encompasses the organizational norms, values and practices that promote continuous learning, experimentation and knowledge-sharing among employees. For example, if your organization values risk-taking, then your employees should be incentivized, not penalized, for trying new and innovative ways of doing things. In those situations where attempts do not result in new and improved outcomes, you must have the tolerance to accept these inevitable failures as a natural outcome of the learning process. Furthermore, if you are continuously engaged in learning as a team and organization, you will have feedback loops built into concept models or early prototypes.

There is another benefit of learning from trying something new, even if it does not work out. For example, if a new partnership fails to meet intended outcomes on a specific initiative, there may be benefits or unintended positive outcomes to having built a solid relationship, like continuing to share resources. If you can reframe a failed attempt and adopt a learning mindset, there are many lessons to be learned.

Team and organizational learning

Team learning fosters collective growth and innovation through shared experiences, insights and feedback. Organizational success hinges on the ability of teams to collaborate, learn from failures and leverage diverse perspectives to drive performance and achieve strategic objectives.

At Organizations by Design Inc. in the summer of 2025, we embarked on building an ambitious Customer Relationship Management platform. This 10-week project, on top of our regular operations, with a new staff member and a summer intern, was certainly one of those opportunities to learn and grow together. The learning curve was steep for all of us but we kept up with a gifted platform development consultant, providing us with a perfect opportunity to build our team learning, learn about each other and integrate the newer team members into our organization.

Learning together requires key values like humility, empathy, consistency, courage and trust. By fostering an environment of trust, psychological safety and open communication, as a leader you can unleash the full potential of your teams and drive collective success.

It's also important to have a process for sharing things that you are learning with others in your organization. If you can find ways to share what you are learning, you will be able to leverage that information to move forward faster. This will allow you to continuously improve and innovate, keeping you ahead of your competition.

By putting feedback processes in place and using tools such as the **After Action Review** and systems or platforms like Clickup, Trello or Miro to share knowledge and event evaluations, as a leader you can foster a culture of continuous learning and excellence. And this will keep your organization on the leading edge of innovation.

Systems thinking

Another dimension of building a learning culture is systems thinking. This is a holistic approach to problem-solving and analysis that views complex issues as interconnected parts of a system rather than isolated parts. It enables you as a leader to understand the interdependencies within your organizations. By adopting a holistic perspective and recognizing the ripple effects of decisions and actions, as a leader you can better navigate complexities and drive systemic change. A great example of this is spending time looking at the impact that a strategic decision can have on parts of the organization. Then you must anticipate some things that might need to be addressed prior to an announcement — and how you will message that decision.

However, sometimes the way things should be done are not the way things are done. A feminine-inspired leader pushes deeper to examine the mindsets that uphold the system and the deep beliefs and values that created them. If you are looking to do that, a really helpful tool is the **Systems Iceberg Model**.

Coaching and a coach approach

Coaching plays a pivotal role in facilitating individual and team development, fostering self-awareness and unlocking potential. By providing guidance, feedback and support, leadership coaches empower individuals to identify their strengths, address weaknesses and achieve their professional goals.

Coaching is a catalyst for personal and professional growth, but you don't have to have a coaching designation to adopt a coach's approach when you are leading teams.

Coaching at its basic level is the process of teaching people how to learn and generate solutions or a path forward. By adopting a coaching philosophy, investing in coaching programs or taking a coach's approach, your organization can cultivate a culture of continuous learning, feedback and improvement. A great resource for integrating a coach approach is ***Humble Inquiry: The Gentle Art of Asking Instead of Telling*** by Dr. Edgar H. Schein, one of the gurus of organizational learning.

Diverse perspectives

Another key dimension of creating a learning culture is a diverse team. One of the elements of diversity that is often overlooked is diversity of perspective and worldview. I highly recommend hiring not just for diversity in the areas that are most often cited, but to intentionally bring in individuals who think differently from the status quo or hold a different worldview.

Embracing diversity and diverse perspectives enriches an organizational learning culture, fosters innovation and enhances problem-solving capabilities. By valuing and fully leveraging the unique insights and experiences of individuals from diverse backgrounds as members of your teams, you can drive creativity, resilience and competitive advantage.

Diversity is not just a moral imperative; it is a strategic advantage. By cultivating an inclusive culture where diverse voices are heard and valued, leaders like you can unlock new opportunities, drive innovation and foster a culture of belonging. You need to create a place where people are excited about coming to work every day, feel valued and are motivated to provide their contributions to the team. This results in a workplace where staff engagement, motivation, attendance and satisfaction are high, and there is a lineup of people who want to be a part of this kind of dynamic learning team and organization.

When we get caught up in doing things the way we have always done them and are not open to new perspectives, we stay stuck and this can hamper our ability to stay on the leading edge in our industries.

As a leader, I highly recommend that you tap into the full potential of your team. They will rise at every occasion given to share their perspective, ideas and expertise. Do this by encouraging open dialogue, asking good questions and remaining curious about different viewpoints. When people feel it is safe to contribute their ideas, teams become more creative and collaborative. They learn better together. And this fosters an environment where people feel valued and empowered to contribute.

The importance of evaluation

As noted in the chapter introduction, evaluation is an essential dimension for assessing the effectiveness and impact of learning initiatives and interventions. By collecting feedback, analyzing data and measuring outcomes, you can identify areas for improvement, optimize performance and drive continuous learning and growth. An example would be to do pre- and post-assessments on clients attending a program and to set up the measures to align with the intended program outcomes.

By incorporating evaluation mechanisms such as formal assessments, project evaluations and after-action reviews, leaders can ensure that learning initiatives align with organizational goals and priorities. It does not have to be complicated. It just requires that we are feeding back what we are learning, making course corrections, repeating the things that are working well and changing the things that are not working.

Reframing and self-reflection tools

Reframing is a powerful tool. It involves shifting perspectives and challenging assumptions to see situations and challenges in a new light. By reframing obstacles as opportunities and failures as learning experiences, as a leader you can cultivate a growth mindset and foster resilience and innovation.

Reframing empowers you to adopt a more constructive outlook on challenges and setbacks. By encouraging reframing techniques and mindset shifts, you can create a learning team and an organizational learning culture where resilience, adaptability and innovation thrive. For example, those conversations that you find difficult to have with an employee — like addressing unmet expectations — can be reframed as a development opportunity. If together you can identify the barriers and put resources in place to support the individual, you turn this into a growth opportunity.

Self-reflection is another powerful tool and practice. It's essential for personal and professional growth, enabling individuals to gain insights into their thoughts, feelings and behaviours. By engaging in regular self-reflection as a leader and building this in as a practice with your teams, you remain in a growth-oriented and learning mindset.

By taking the time to reflect on our experiences, behaviours and decisions, you can identify areas for growth, develop new perspectives, and enhance your effectiveness as leaders and teams.

This can involve building in simple questions on a meeting agenda, such as:

- "What did we learn about x from our meeting yesterday with our partner?"
- "What do we want to stop, start or continue doing to improve our team relationships?"
- "What would we do differently the next time we host this annual event to increase attendance, engagement or impact?"

As you can see, the questions create the iterative learning.

Ground rules for creating a learning team

I want to end this chapter covering the ground rules that need to be in place to create a learning environment. Now that you have read the chapter, you are better-positioned to understand why these ground rules are so important. Here they are:

- Create a psychologically safe learning environment because high levels of team trust are key to building a learning team.

- Make openness and trust the rule because it is important for people to feel secure enough to speak freely, without fear of reprisal, but also within the rules of engagement (which is covered in the chapter on trust) you have created together.
- Agree that remarks participants make will not be attributed to them outside of the group unless they consent. And ensure that conversations outside of the team, which impact team trust, will be brought back into the team. For example, if you are talking about the impact of a team member's behaviour (e.g. failure to meet time-sensitive deadlines), it's imperative that you bring that back into the team conversations. Likewise, if you are speaking about an amazing presentation that a team member did and they are not present, then bring that back into the team conversation too. Dr. Beth Page, one of my Royal Roads University professors, refers to this as honouring the absent. This is a key to sustaining team trust.
- Encourage and reward the injection of new perspectives but not the selling of them. By this, I mean encouraging people to make contributions and share ideas, but do not pitch them as 'the answer.' Throw them into the mix and see what happens. And once the team has come to consensus on how to move forward, let go of the pieces that you presented but were not adopted. Being in solidarity with your teammates and the team decisions is good practice.
- Expect that the focus will be on the work and the decisions, not on the person. Don't personalize or tie a team member's idea to who they are, but rather, acknowledge the contributions they are making to advance the work.

Fostering a culture of learning is not merely a strategic imperative — it is the lifeblood of organizational excellence and resilience. By embracing a holistic approach to learning that encompasses individual development, team dynamics and organizational processes, as a leader you can create an environment where curiosity, innovation, learning and collaboration thrive.

As you navigate the complexities of the modern business landscape, remember that learning is not a destination but a journey — one of exploration, discovery and growth. By cultivating a culture of learning, you can empower your teams to adapt, evolve and thrive.

🔍 Reflection Questions

1. **What are the current learning habits or patterns in my organization or team?**

   In what ways do these support or inhibit innovation, growth, and adaptability?

   _____

   _____

   _____

   _____

   _____

2. **How do I personally respond to failure or mistakes?**

   Do you see them as opportunities for learning—or sources of blame and defensiveness?

   _____

   _____

   _____

   _____

   _____

3. **To what extent am I practising systems thinking in my leadership role?**

   Can you think of a recent challenge where using systems thinking might have changed your response or decision?

   _____

   _____

   _____

   _____

   _____

4. **Do my team members feel psychologically safe enough to ask questions, challenge assumptions or share new ideas?**

   How are you actively creating or reinforcing this environment?

   _____

   _____

   _____

   _____

   _____

CHAPTER 6

Thinking Way Beyond Black and White

In your busy workplace, the greatest gift you can give yourself as a leader is some thinking time. It will make you more efficient in the long run. The quality of your thinking and thinking processes has a direct impact on your communication, decision-making and ultimately your results.

One of my leadership clients, Shar, shared in a strategic thinking session that her calendar was filled with back-to-back meetings, constant decisions and endless interruptions. She was doing everything — except thinking clearly. As the pace quickened during her busy season, she felt the pressure more acutely. A quick hiring decision was creating tension amongst the team and a surge in customer complaints. She described spending more time putting out fires than focusing on the tasks that were most important. I challenged her to find two hours a week for some deep thinking. No interruptions. No meetings. No emails. That small shift changed everything. She became more strategic and less reactive. Her communication improved. Decisions became deliberate, not rushed. In our next session, she shared that those two hours saved her 10.

It's also all too easy to fall into patterns of conventional thinking — to default to familiar strategies and approaches without questioning whether they are still effective. Innovation and growth come from a willingness to challenge the status quo — to question assumptions, explore alternative perspectives and embrace new ideas.

In today's fast-paced business world, where challenges can be complex and solutions aren't always clear, strong, well-developed thinking skills can significantly increase your effectiveness as a leader. This chapter explores what thinking means for leaders, offering clear definitions, common language, insights and practical tools. It explores the important role thinking plays in helping leaders, their teams and organizations succeed.

Thinking: definition, shared language and meaning

Thinking is how we process information to understand the world around us. It includes both conscious and subconscious ways of analyzing ideas, experiences and information. It shapes how we see situations. There are different ways we can use and hone our thinking skills as leaders.

Strategic thinking is the masculine learning lens through which many business decisions are made — a primarily linear process that looks at how we can use our people and resources to get to where we want to be. It takes in many traditional pieces of information using tools like **SWOT** and **PESTLE** to mitigate the risks and understand the opportunities within various aspects of the current business environment. We develop strategic plans and then we work the plan.

Systems Thinking is a way of seeing the relationship among systems, whether that is the organization you work in, or the organization you work in within the sector, or within the local community that includes other businesses. Think about it like a telephoto camera lens — you can zoom in or out. You can look at the way parts of the systems interact and impact one another rather than focusing narrowly on the parts themselves. Systems thinking is a perspective, a philosophy, a language, a set of tools and a body of knowledge. In a world of complex systems, it's a way to find small, strategic changes that can lead to significant impacts.

There are two other thinking skills you need to understand — filters and the mental processes we use to make sense of the situations in which we find ourselves and the world around us.

Let me begin with a story. I met Yvonne in my *Leadership Edmonton* cohort and recall her sharing a visual about the filters through which we see the world. Filters like our worldview, our lived experiences, our beliefs, orientation, attitudes etc. Filters that result in people seeing the same situation differently. This is at play every day in the workplace, which is the reason communication is so critical, and why checking in with individuals and teams to verify their understanding is so important.

But taking in information is just one part. The second part is the mental process we use to make sense of the situation. And the third part is what we end up doing or not doing with that information. You may recall that amazing tool called the **Ladder of Inference** that was introduced in the communications chapter. It is a mental model, developed by organizational psychologist Dr. Chris Argyris, that outlines the rapid process our minds go through to draw conclusions and take action in a given situation.

The importance of mental models

Mental Models are the mental frameworks or "maps" we use to understand the world, make decisions and solve problems. Think of them as the invisible rules or patterns we've learned from past experiences, beliefs and cultural influences. They shape how we see situations, interpret information and decide what to do next.

But here's the key: mental models aren't set in stone. As leaders, we can refine and expand these models through self-reflection, learning and by exposing ourselves to different perspectives. By doing this we make better decisions, empathize more deeply and adapt to changing circumstances.

Imagine you're in a team meeting and a discussion gets heated. Your mental model — based on your past experiences — might tell you "Conflict is bad; we need to shut this down." But what if you challenge that model? By questioning your assumption and seeing conflict as an opportunity for growth, you could guide the conversation toward creative problem-solving instead by using the ladder of inference which explains how we process information, often without realizing it. Here's how it works:

1. **Observing:** You take in raw data (like hearing someone raise their voice.)
2. **Selecting:** You focus on specific details (e.g. "They seem upset.")
3. **Interpreting:** You apply meaning based on your mental model ("They're angry because they don't agree with me.")
4. **Concluding:** You make a judgment ("They don't value my opinion.")
5. **Acting:** You decide how to respond (e.g. "I'll stop sharing my ideas.")

This process happens quickly, almost automatically, but it's not always accurate. By pausing to reflect on each step, you can uncover assumptions and choose actions that align with your leadership goals. As noted in the client story in an earlier chapter, your time spent thinking can save you minutes or hours later, and given that time is a resource, as a leader you want to use your resources effectively.

Challenging and refining your mental models is like upgrading your toolkit as a leader. The more diverse and adaptable your mental models, the better equipped you'll be to handle complex situations with clarity and confidence.

Embracing adaptive thinking

You know that change is a constant in today's fast-moving world of business. New technologies, shifting markets and organizational challenges mean that as a leader, you need to think on your feet and stay flexible. This is where adaptive thinking comes in. It's the ability to learn, adjust and find new ways forward when the unexpected happens.

Adaptive thinking is about more than just reacting to change. It's about staying one step ahead. By staying curious and open to new ideas, you can spot emerging trends, turn challenges into opportunities and avoid potential risks. For example, imagine a company is facing a sudden drop in customer demand. A leader with adaptive thinking would explore innovative solutions, such as launching a new product or changing how services are delivered, rather than sticking rigidly to old strategies.

This way of thinking also creates a ripple effect within teams. When leaders encourage flexibility, experimentation and collaboration, they build a culture where people feel confident trying new approaches and solving problems together. Teams that embrace change can tackle challenges more effectively, bounce back from setbacks, and help their organizations grow — even in tough times.

To thrive in today's unpredictable world, you need to see change not as a threat but as an opportunity to learn, grow and innovate. There is a whole chapter on change endurance and change management in this book. By fostering adaptive thinking in yourself and your teams, you can navigate uncertainty with confidence and create success.

Disconnect between leaders' and team thinking

One common challenge in leadership is the disconnect that can exist between you and your team. This gap often happens because you each see things differently, have distinct communication styles or operate under varying assumptions about how things should work. But this diversity of perspective can actually be an asset, not a liability.

For instance, a leader might assume their team agrees with a decision because no one raises objections in a meeting. However, team members might hesitate to speak up, thinking their ideas conflict with the leader's vision. Or they may be too introverted to speak up unless you as a leader invite them and create space for them to share. This disconnect can lead to missed opportunities for innovation or problem-solving. When leaders actively encourage diverse perspectives, it not only bridges the gap but also helps uncover valuable insights that might otherwise go unspoken.

To bridge this gap, leaders need to focus on open dialogue and active participation. This means creating opportunities for everyone to share their perspectives, ask questions and contribute ideas.

Bridging the gap isn't just about solving problems — it's about creating a culture where everyone feels valued and heard, where there are opportunities for meaningful engagement and contribution. When you and your team are on the same page, it fosters collaboration, boosts morale and engagement and drives better results for everyone.

Transparency is another key ingredient. When you openly share your thinking and reasoning, it helps build trust and alignment. For instance, a leader who explains the "why" behind a decision can help team members see the rationale, so they are more informed, understand better and feel more connected to the plan or directive. They also see the alignment with the organization's mission. It is helpful particularly for newer team members to connect the dots between current actions and future goals.

Use integrative thinking

Integrative thinking is a fancy way of asking how, as leaders, do we bring together differing perspectives and ideas to develop innovative solutions to complex problems?

The most straightforward way is encouraging reflective learning and asking probing questions. This is a way you can foster critical thinking within your team. In strategic-thinking sessions with our client leaders, I often get to a place where we have a conversation about coaching versus telling. Using a coach approach is about guiding your team or team member through a learning process to cultivate their thinking skills. If you have a tendency to be a directive hands-on (read micromanaging) leader or have low trust in your team or you do a lot of telling and have team members consistently coming to you for direction, consider shifting to a coach approach.

I hired an assistant and the differentiating factor that set her apart was her desire to be continuously learning. She was young, so sought out coaching to be able to reflect and distill the lessons she was learning. In our regular one-on-one sessions we would start with the highlights, accomplishments and wins since our last session. Next we addressed setbacks. Through a series of focused coaching questions, she gained tremendous insights into an unhealthy work pattern. After those insights she applied some sound strategies that she had generated to address this pattern and has grown to be an invaluable member of our team.

Another way to activate integrative thinking is by creating safe workspaces where it is all right to challenge assumptions, explore alternative viewpoints and ask powerful questions. In the chapter on trust, I take a deep dive into creating trust and building psychologically safe workspaces.

Begin with your thinking

Leadership isn't just about what you do; it's about how you think. Whether you're crafting a vision, solving a tough problem or building trust with your team, the quality of your thinking will always define the quality of your results.

As a leader, don't settle for the comfort of conventional thinking. Instead, take a moment to pause, question assumptions and explore new perspectives. Lean into complexity. Know that your approach to thinking — strategic, systemic and inclusive — sets the tone for decisions, actions and the ripple effects those actions create.

And remember, strong thinking isn't just about you — it's a team advantage. By encouraging open dialogue, balancing advocacy with inquiry and welcoming diverse perspectives, you can create an environment where your team thrives.

At its core, your leadership is about imagining what's possible and inspiring others to make it real. Thinking is the foundation of this vision. It gives you the clarity to navigate uncertainty, the courage to challenge the status quo, and the wisdom to connect with your team and stakeholders in meaningful ways.

So, as you move forward, take this to heart: your thinking shapes your leadership, and your leadership shapes the future. Make time for it. Refine it. Cultivate it. Use it not just to lead, but to inspire, empower and create lasting impact.

Lead with intention, purpose and vision, one thoughtful decision at a time.

Effective leadership begins with intentional, high-quality thinking. As a leader, your ability to challenge assumptions, embrace diverse perspectives and balance advocacy with inquiry sets the foundation for your success. By refining mental models, fostering adaptive thinking and cultivating strategic and systems thinking, you can navigate complexities with clarity and confidence. Remember, the way you think influences not only your decisions but also the culture of your team. Create space for dialogue, encourage innovative solutions and inspire others to think boldly. Leadership is a ripple effect — let your thinking be the spark that drives meaningful change and lasting impact.

🔍 Reflection Questions

1. **When was the last time I created uninterrupted space to think deeply — not just react — about a challenge I'm facing? What shifted as a result?**

   Explore the impact of intentional thinking time on your leadership clarity and decision-making.

   _____
   _____
   _____
   _____
   _____

2. **What mental models might be shaping how I currently view a person, problem or project — and are those models still serving me and my team?**

   Challenge assumptions and bring unconscious frameworks into conscious awareness.

   _____
   _____
   _____
   _____
   _____

3. **How often do I seek out — and genuinely consider — perspectives that are different from my own?**

   Reflect on your openness to diverse thinking and how it influences your team culture.

   _____
   _____
   _____
   _____
   _____

4. **Do I encourage strategic and systems thinking in my team or am I stuck in a pattern of "telling" rather than coaching?**

   Examine your leadership approach and how it shapes others' capacity to think and act.

   _____
   _____
   _____
   _____
   _____

5. **What changes could I make to foster a stronger thinking culture across my team or organization?**

   Consider concrete actions like scheduling reflection time, hosting "thinking sessions" or using tools like the Ladder of Inference or Iceberg Model.

   _____

   _____

   _____

   _____

   _____

CHAPTER 7

Relationship Intelligence — Leading Through Connection, Not Control

Managing relationships takes effort and commitment.

Having healthy relationships with colleagues at work is key to effective leadership. And managing boundaries and being transparent about relationships with colleagues outside of work is essential to avoid creating unhealthy team dynamics or subgroups within your team or organization.

It's important to have clear standards about our expectations and about bringing things that happen between co-workers outside the workplace back into the team. Dr. Beth Page, refers to this practice as honouring the absent in her book *Change Happens,* which we explored in the chapter on change and transition. Dr. Beth Page advises, whether we are having positive discussions about one of our peers (e.g. wasn't that an amazing presentation so and so did with that client group?) or are vocalizing concerns (e.g. is her pattern of late deadline delivering impacting you as much as me?), we must bring those conversations back to the team because they have an impact on team relationships. When as leaders we create psychologically safe workspaces and have clearly defined shared commitments, this just seamlessly integrates into the way we work together.

And if you are wondering about those situations where there is a pre-existing relationship (e.g. you have worked together at another company or you were friends prior to the start of the work relationship), it's important to let the team know that too. My business partner hired a supervisor from a former agency where they had worked together, and they were friends. Being transparent with the team, and letting them know that they both committed to following the protocols outlined above, ensured that if either positive or concerning conversations came up outside of work, that they would keep the rest of the team in the know. This piece of advice can save you a lot of unnecessary strife and clarity on expectations.

Develop a relationship with each team member

As a leader, you should be meeting with each member of your team (direct reports) on a regular basis. You get to define what regular means (daily, weekly, monthly). It depends on a few factors, including the nature and pace of your work (intensive-care nurses do this multiple times on a shift). It depends on the tenure of your report; usually the longer you have had this relationship, the less frequent and shorter these meetings can be. And with new team members, you may meet more often initially and then taper to the intervals that you meet with your other staff. Again, it depends on the level of independence and need for input, which varies from employee to employee.

The frequency and length of your meetings will vary with the type of work and what is happening in the workplace. For example, highly time-sensitive projects may require more frequent touchpoints, whereas during periods when things are slow, you might meet less often. So there are many permeations, but the important takeaway is to give each team member some of your one-on-one time. It's critical to building your relationship to touch base on the status of work tasks, to determine the resources they need to do their work (more people, more time, more room, more money) and the barriers they are running into (delays from other areas, difficult-to-manage customers, etc.)

These sessions should happen throughout the employee life cycle, from the first day they start until they leave the organization. As their leader, your primary role is three-fold:

- Get to know them in many ways. What assets do they bring to the table? What are they passionate about? What motivates them? What do they enjoy outside of work? What are their values? In short, get to know them as people.
- Provide them with the resources they need to do their job well (e.g. staff, training, space etc.)
- Have them identify the barriers they are running into (e.g. difficult co-worker, supply chain disruptions, confidence etc.) Either brainstorm solutions, assisting them in overcoming barriers, or remove those barriers for them (e.g., facilitating a meeting, supporting a new supplier, etc.)

As far as the structure of these touchpoints, connection points or meetings, make time for a bit of the personal, then focus on resources and barriers to assist them in doing their jobs.

And remember, you are always managing expectations, explicitly or implicitly, in every conversation or meeting, in all your work relationships. Model the way you want people to be together through the way you engage with others and how you show up each and every day. This is a big part in leading the way.

Investing time and energy into building relationships

It's important that we know each other as people to be most effective in our work together.

Investing time and energy into building authentic workplace relationships can take many forms, including one-on-one meetings, project teams, team-building or learning events, to name just a few. I like taking time as a leader to provide opportunities for team members to showcase their preferred work style or their communication style or their personalities to build relationships and understanding about the different approaches we take to our work as individuals. It's important to value diversity and understand it, rather than seek conformity.

Look for opportunities that present themselves and intentionally create a sense of camaraderie and belonging through intentional interactions. One way is to build in an open question on every other agenda to increase that understanding and awareness of each other. It's even better if it is organic and directly related to the task. Here's an example: "Given the situation that we are in with this client, I am interested in hearing how each of you would communicate our concerns?" As the team lead, proceed to facilitate a roundtable discussion, hearing from everyone. This is a way for everyone to see their teammates' communication style in play, and to teach what's OK in the work culture along the way. And at the end of the discussion, come to a consensus on which approach might garner the most desirable outcome. This is a great example that also looks at balancing the task and relationship-building that was addressed in the last section.

There are many assessment or team-building awareness exercises like the **MBTI** or **Team Dynamics** available and they don't have to involve a day-long endeavour, although team-building days are important too. I have listed a few of my favourites in the chapter resource section. Integrate them into your team activities and watch the difference it makes when people know and understand one another as individuals, not just the roles they play in the organization.

A balance between work and play goes a long way

Whatever you do, never underestimate the value of making time to foster personal connections in and outside the workplace to strengthen team dynamics. All work and no play is a recipe for failure, burnout, disengagement and high turnover rates. After all, these are humans you lead and keep in mind they have social needs that need to be satisfied.

There is no prescription for the perfect event; you have to figure that out with and make that happen for your team. One of my clients has a monthly staff event that revolves around food. Staff members have a set budget and take turns planning a different lunch, which has ranged from a food truck to a BBQ to a multicultural meal and more. It's a time to just be together, to enjoy the food, to learn about each other as people, and to not talk about work!

Some people are naturally drawn to other staff, and friendships form outside of work due to mutual passions (e.g. running, young moms, etc.) And as long as you have set the standards outlined at the beginning of this chapter, that works. On a personal note, I curated an anthology called *__Creating Connections: How Friendships Feed the Soul__*. More than half of the co-authors are people I met at work and maintained a relationship with after one or both of us left to pursue other opportunities. I believe that creating connections is important personally and in the workplace. If you are looking for inspiring stories, then get the book at Amazon.ca

The heart of relationship-building

Make time to get to know each of the human beings you lead. Knowing their strengths, preferred work style, personality, motivations, passions and a few things about their personal life is important to finding the best strategies and approach to lead them. One of my clients who leads a large team, puts birthday reminders for her direct reports in her calendar so she can do something small yet thoughtful for them on that day. These gestures will also help you support them in being high-performing members of the team and in doing exceptional work.

The 2020 COVID-19 pandemic tore down the barriers between work and home. Through the magic of Zoom and other platforms, we got to see our colleagues in their homes, to experience their reality and their struggles. And this continues for those working in virtual environments. Whether your team is working virtually or in person, one of the most powerful things you can convey as a leader is your understanding of who your people are, to see them is vital. Being able to connect with them. For them to know that you understand them, appreciate them for the unique person that they are, and that you value their contributions is at the heart of relationship-building.

As a leader, you need a clear picture of not only their current state and the things that are important to them, but also how they want to grow, so that you can provide them with those opportunities within your organization. In short, hold onto these valuable resources, who we sometimes forget in the busyness of the work. Remember that they are human beings and our most valuable resource, and without them we would not be able to do the work.

In one of my roles, as a new area director for a home-health agency, our receptionist was on the cusp of being let go by the regional director. During my onboarding, the regional director shared the concerns that had been documented by the agency, and said one of my tasks was to figure out a way forward or to replace the employee. I told her that I wanted a chance to get to know this person, to hear her story. As we built our relationship, the employee shared her future goal, which was to get a nursing designation. The intensity of her studies and class schedule had been impacting her work. I told her that I would support her in reaching her goal and that we could look at a more flexible schedule. There was a 180-degree change in her behaviour and she became a model employee, with a revised schedule that worked for us and allowed her to pursue her studies. Together, we found a way to align personal and organizational goals. We retained a valuable employee, saved on turnover costs, and built an allegiance that would one day enable us to employ her in an alternate capacity, as a nurse!

The importance of emotional intelligence

Emotional intelligence (EI) or emotional quotient (EQ) is a concept that was introduced in the 1990s by authors like Daniel Goleman. It is just as relevant, if not more so today, and an important leadership skill if you are leading people.

EI is the ability to understand your emotions and the emotions of those around you in the workspace. Being self-aware and being able to demonstrate your own vulnerability and to share your feelings provides your team with permission to do the same with you and other stakeholders. Taking an **EI assessment** to identify your strengths and gap areas is a good place to start. Doing this will make you more aware as a leader and more attuned to others.

As we will learn in the chapter on change management, assisting employees to identify and work through their feelings about change, big or small, is the key to having them transition to the desired future state. Our emotions have a lot of sway when it comes to our thoughts about different things, and we act out in ways that are aligned with our emotions. This has the potential to move us forward or to regress. Think about the possibility of using EI as a leader. This would allow you to understand the emotions we all experience during our day and use them to provide you with insight and to make decisions as a leader.

Benefits of building strategic alliances

In the interconnected landscape of leadership, strategic alliances serve as invaluable resources for collaboration and growth. By leveraging external partnerships and fostering collaborations, leaders can tap into a wealth of knowledge and expertise, enriching their leadership journey and enhancing team and organizational effectiveness. Strategic alliances provide avenues for learning and opportunities that extend beyond the confines of the organization.

Take, for example, the C5 initiative between five non-profit agencies in Edmonton, Alberta, Canada that collectively serve over 13,000 clients annually. They have shared services, such as a human resource recruitment officer who posts, screens and sets up interviews with candidates for vacant positions for all five of the organizations in this collaborative. Another shared service is mandatory sector training, which they offer jointly multiple times annually to ensure all staff have choices for training dates. They also offer an annual all-agency training event. It's fun and they share or take turns in planning the event, leveraging valuable resources and time. In addition, they host joint meetings at various levels of leadership (executive director, senior leaders, managers) at set times to provide opportunities to share best practices and cross-pollinate ideas.

Trust: the foundation of authentic relationships

At the core of authentic relationships lies trust, which underpins every interaction and decision between individuals in and outside our teams and organizations. From times of agreement to moments of disagreement, trust enables team members to share their perspectives openly, without fear of reprisal.

Psychological safety is the linchpin upon which trust is built. By creating an environment where team members feel valued, respected and supported, leaders lay the foundation for collaboration, innovation and growth.

Knowing about the importance of trust and psychological safety is one thing, but having the capacity to create a psychologically safe environment is another. For that reason, I have dedicated an entire chapter to ways to build trust and including creating psychological safe workspaces.

Navigating leadership through relationships

Relationships are the cornerstone of effective leadership. So as you navigate the complexities of leadership, always remember the profound impact authentic relationships have on shaping your team and organization. I have learned that anything is possible when, as leaders, we value relationships with the people with whom we work each day and acknowledge the profound impact of authentic human relationships on our organizational success.

Some leaders with whom I have worked over the years have told me stories about how they rose to heights in their organizations by putting their people first and valuing their contributions. This helped them to support their organizations during times of crisis and need. I worked with an all-women senior leadership team, and while facilitating our Systems Leadership program, they shared that they felt the strongest bond as a team when they were able to tap into the unique skill sets of team members. They were able to do this as a result of having built relationships, both individually and as a team, during times of stress, like their move to a new office space.

If you embrace a leadership approach rooted in human connection and trust, the payoffs are great and it makes the work so much more satisfying, innovative and meaningful.

When you prioritize relationships and lead with emotional intelligence, you empower your team to innovate, grow and face challenges with confidence. True success isn't about individual accomplishments; it's about the collective effort and the bonds that strengthen and inspire your team. This is the power of feminine-inspired leadership, a leadership approach that can transform how you work together with others, creating lasting impact and fulfillment for everyone involved.

🔍 Reflection Questions

1. **How am I currently investing time and energy into building authentic relationships with each team member?**

   Consider your frequency of one-on-ones, the depth of conversations and how well you understand their motivations, strengths and challenges.

   _____

   _____

   _____

   _____

2. **In what ways do I model transparency and set clear boundaries around relationships, especially regarding interactions outside of work?**

   Reflect on whether your team understands how external relationships impact team dynamics and if expectations are clear to prevent subgroups or misunderstandings.

   _____

   _____

   _____

   _____

3. **How do I create psychological safety within my team to encourage open dialogue, diverse perspectives and risk-taking?**

   Think about your actions, language and reactions in meetings or informal interactions—do they invite trust and honest communication?

   _____

   _____

   _____

   _____

   _____

4. **When faced with conflicts or barriers within my team, how do I approach resolution in a way that strengthens relationships rather than damages them?**

   Reflect on your mindset, communication style, and how you balance task completion with preserving or rebuilding trust.

   _____

   _____

   _____

   _____

   _____

5. What small, consistent behaviours or rituals can I adopt to deepen connection, build camaraderie and celebrate the unique contributions of each team member?

   Consider actions like recognizing birthdays, facilitating team-sharing moments or creating informal social events that nurture belonging.

   _____

   _____

   _____

   _____

   _____

CHAPTER 8

Leading Through Change and Transition

You likely feel the impacts of changes in your external environment, on your organization, your teams and yourself. These could be anything from new work configurations and downsizing to adopting artificial intelligence in the workplace. It's a lot when the landscape that you are working in fluctuates every day.

In this chapter, I will address both change and transition. It's important to differentiate between them — change is an event, and transition is the psychological process in response to the change event. I will explore transition as a key in the change-management process and the importance of making it our new normal. I will offer strategies for leading through change and share a proven framework for change management that is called the 5C model.

I'm sure you have heard the saying that the only constant today is change. Ironically, the Greek philosopher Heraclitus said the very same thing — 2,500 years ago! Yet we all feel that change is different today. It's been described as relentless, continuous, wall-to-wall, non-stop. I hear from client leaders that the pace of information and change is so fast, they feel overwhelmed and find it hard to keep up. So if you sometimes feel this way, you are not alone. We need to talk not of *a* single change but of change as an ongoing phenomenon. As a collage, not a simple image: one change overlaps with another, and it's all change as far as the eye can see. You can see why that would feel overwhelming at times.

Organizations need to change

Growth and change are a normal part of every leader and organization's evolution. And if we fail to adjust to rapidly changing environments both internally and externally, our organizations might very well cease to exist, like Kodak, which did not see the future of digital photography. As a leader it is critical that you manage those changes, in ways that allow your organization to continue not only to survive but to thrive.

And in today's world of non-stop change, effective strategies for managing change are not just a 'nice to have' but 'a need to have' for all leaders. Futurists suggest that we will experience 100 years of change in the next decade. So even if you see yourself as a good change leader, sharpening your change endurance and change resilience capabilities will serve you well moving forward at an accelerated pace.

Before jumping into strategies for leading through change, let's look at your view of change. Do you see it as a disruption? A never-ending roller-coaster ride? Is it exhilarating or exhausting? What if you viewed change as an opportunity for growth and innovation? How might that influence how you currently manage change?

Defining change

Your definition of change matters.

I define change as an event or situation that takes place: a new CEO, moving to a new office space, a new arm of the business, moving from an old to a new IT platform. These events occur as the organization strives for desired outcomes, usually related to outside factors, such as customer preference, regulatory changes, new competitors or needed expansion to meet demand.

As a leader you are likely well-trained to manage the tasks that are required of 'the change' but do you understand the importance of managing the impact of the change on people? In my MBA specialization in Leadership & Organizational Development, I acquired a number of tools that were worth the price of tuition. One of them was **Bridges' Model of Transition.**

Dr. William Bridges was an American organizational consultant who referred to transitions as the psychological process that people go through as they come to terms with the new situation that change brings about. His model provides a big insight about why most change efforts fail. People leaders are unaware of the impact that the transition from the old to the new has both psychologically and emotionally on members of their teams. And they don't realize that supporting people is essential in getting them through the transition.

If employees have been involved in building a part of the team or organization that is now being dismantled, it's only reasonable that there would be some feelings associated with the loss, whether they are expressed at work or not. It is essential that you acknowledge that this is happening, have structures and trusted advisers to deal with those psychological responses, like trusted advisers and support people in grieving and leaving the old situation behind. Thus as people leaders, managing transitions should always be central to how you manage the changes in play. It's all explained in the Bridges Transition Model.

Being able to differentiate between change and transition is a valuable concept. It reminds you to appreciate the role of honouring the human dimension of change. As a leader, by understanding transitions; by being a trusted adviser; by acknowledging the endings and associated emotions, by asking good questions and listening deeply, you will be well equipped to lead through changes successfully.

Ironically, one of the reasons organizations have paid so little attention to transition is that they're overwhelmed by it. Transition is all around them — so close that they can't see it clearly. It's not until it's isolated in its simplest form that it can be seen clearly.

Now, let's explore more strategies for managing transitions.

Decision-making

You might wonder why of all things, decision-making would be identified as a strategy for managing change and transition. And the short answer is we need to have clarity on who has authority to make which decisions and the parameters for decision-making. If not, when we are in the midst of a change or simultaneous change events, your people won't have the agility nor feel they have the authority to make good decisions that support the organization in moving forward.

Decision-making usually ties into an individual's role, their scope of responsibility and their accountability. As an organization, it's usually a good idea to have clarity on the decision-making rules and to craft related policies and standards of practice. I took a course on participatory decision making from organizational expert Dr. Sam Kaner, whose book ***Facilitator's Guide to Participatory Decision-Making*** is a great resource.

Clear decision-making processes and stakeholder involvement will serve you well in making informed, good, strategic choices, especially when navigating through the layers of changes that are the current reality in most organizations. There are a ton of tools available but we are going to focus on the ones that I use with my clients, the ones that work.

Role descriptions

Having clearly defined role descriptions that include decision-making authority is important. Role descriptions provide clarity and allow individuals in those roles to know and use the scope of their decision-making power. This allows for quick decision-making that is in alignment with the change initiative and the organization's strategic directives, vision, mission and values. Create practice guidelines and principles that allow them to make decisions. A simple example is a policy where any team member can spend up to $100 on program supplies without prior approval.

Putting these foundations in place allows you and your team members to take calculated risk, to not be risk-averse, and to avoid analysis paralysis. These are all good practices when we need to be agile in a sea of change. Leaders need to collect good data and make decisions with the best information they have at the moment to allow the organization to continue to move forward and not stagnate.

Using this approach will assist you in making good decisions. Often, when as a leader you are at the crossroads and need to make a difficult decision that may impact employees or the future of the organization, it is important to share the information that led to this decision and provide support for those impacted.

Once you have given your direct reports the decision-making authority aligned with their roles, you need to empower and allow them to operate independently within the parameters of your policies and practices. Empowerment is a theme that runs throughout this book.

Presence

Being fully present in the moment is something I taught myself to do as a young professional working mom. I honed this skill of being fully present and not distracted by upcoming events or my phone, although then it was attached to the wall in my office. Even during the busiest times in my life, people I was with, felt they were the most important thing in my life, they felt 'heard' and knew that I was fully present.

I remember working full-time and running for office in my local municipality. After my work day I spent evenings door-knocking and weekends at campaign events. I was able to compartmentalize each engagement, whether it was in a team meeting or at the door with a constituent. I intentionally focused on and engaged in discussions with the person or people in my presence. I was not focused on the next meeting or the next event. That is how you create that presence that people feel, by being fully present in each and every moment.

Teaching yourself to be fully present is a good habit to develop. It is the ability to keep your full attention on another person without allowing your thoughts to wander off to your next meeting or being distracted by your phone. It is about giving them your undivided attention and listening to everything they say. It is particularly important when you are supporting an individual, your team or organization through a transition.

Often our work as leaders is to help people see possibilities during this time of transition. Before we can shift them from viewing change as an either/or and move to a place where they can embrace what the change offers, we must honour and value what exists and what is ending.

One of the most powerful strategies of honouring and valuing is through really listening. As a leader you do this by asking significant questions, which can result in you having a deep conversation about the emotions your employees may be experiencing. You need to get people to recognize that they can accept the situation and move forward if they work through these emotions. And that 'the change' is built on the best of our organizational culture, so that we can keep doing what we are doing as an organisation.

Ceremony

Ceremony is required for closure. And by that, I mean the end of something old and the beginning of something new. Ceremony does not have to be expensive or formal, but it needs to be marked. Let me share a powerful example. At a not-for-profit I worked for, a much-loved supervisor was let go due to funding changes. To help with this transition a talking circle was facilitated by the program director. This allowed staff time to process their emotions related to losing that special supervisor. It was a powerful ceremony that allowed staff to openly express their feelings and allowed them to move forward in their work, without her.

Awareness

In the context of managing change we need to practise awareness — that is, truly being aware of the impact of the transition. And sometimes that means slowing down to gauge and address the impact, which can be challenging for some leaders.

Remember that we are dealing with people, and people need to understand and have information about how a change or decision will affect them personally. How we position that change and the language we use affects them. We need to be very aware of how our communication lands with others. Be mindful of what we say and do, ensuring that our words and actions are congruent.

Also remember that those implementing the change will be at a different place in the journey. And each team member will be at a different level. Some will have already moved on, embraced or adopted the change; others will be grieving the loss of the old familiar ways and reluctant to change —

and everyone else will be somewhere in between. As a leader, you need to be really present with those around you, to be mindful of every piece of the process and how it is impacting the whole system.

By considering the potential impacts to the whole system, especially those people it most affects, you can get out in front of it. And keep the conversation going by keeping people in the know. By doing this you'll improve your chances of a successful change outcome and you will be keeping any fallout to a minimum. *Change Happens* and Bridges Transition Model are two great resources.

Deep listening

Another strategy is to lean into your listening, which we covered in our communications chapter. In situations where we are managing change, listen to what is being said and what is not being said at the deepest level. What is not being said is so much more powerful in terms of learning and really understanding. I call it listening around the edges, tuning in to your intuition and senses to really understand what is going on and how people are responding. For example, if you broach a question in an area that is really important to your team, and there is silence, you know they are holding back. And you need to get curious about why they are not being forthcoming.

One of the consistent issues I hear when working with individuals or teams who are struggling through change and transition is that they are not being heard, that they don't have a voice. Listening is all about ensuring that you are hearing both your team's ideas about change and the feelings associated with a change that is not their idea.

Simultaneous change

So what happens when everything is changing or when there are multiple layers of change events happening all at once? To lead through simultaneous change, you need an overall design within which the various and separate changes are integrated as component elements.

As you know, it gets even more complicated, as changes spin off from earlier changes in a never-ending sequence. An example might be that in the changeover to a new client information system, you might also be entering the transition caused by a recently announced reorganization. To make things more challenging, you are right in the middle of dealing with the impact of a new funding model.

Your experience as a leader can be compared to that of someone conducting an orchestra. And you will need a score, written music that integrates all sections of the orchestra. In business terms, you need an overall design within which the various separate changes are integrated as component elements. This is key to integrating non-stop organizational change.

In periods of major strategic change, when the overall new plans, structures and goals are conveyed to the organization by your senior leadership, consider yourself fortunate. For, even if you don't entirely agree with the logic of the larger change, you benefit from the coherence it gives to the component changes. If, on the other hand, no larger strategy exists, you'll need to analyze the changes and discover — or perhaps even invent — their underlying common purpose. These might include:

- The need to save money
- The need to respond creatively to a new government climate
- The need to speed up decision-making by decentralizing authority

As a leader, you need to create a clearer picture of the overarching change that your organization is going through. You have to find a few larger patterns that integrate and make sense out of all the specific changes. When you've done that, you can use it to orchestrate your responses.

Three leadership competencies

Given that seeing into the future is outside of our ability, I recommend focusing on three things that are within our control. Namely, being future-focused, developing change readiness and a change in mindset. These leadership competencies must be developed and are highly sought-after in today's workplace.

Future-focused

Being future-focused can be done through a life-cycle-based approach to these issues, which will give you the lead time to avoid the predictable crisis of having to manage a big transition triggered by a change that no one foresaw. You can be ready with alternatives when the first cracks are discovered. A second way to be ready for the future is to build into every change initiative a "what if?" clause. For example, what if 50 per cent more people than you predicted take you up on the change you are making to your early retirement offer? And what if they're the wrong people, the ones you want to keep? What if a government redesigns how we deliver care in our sector? In other words, what if things don't turn out the way you hope and plan that they will?

Build into all of your plans a contingency clause that suggests what you would do if the unexpected happened. In that way, you will have alternative routes ready to take if the main route is closed unexpectedly, as well as established procedures for changing things up with a minimum of chaos if your plan is undermined by unforeseen events.

Change readiness

As leaders you must shift the culture in ways that will make your organizations more agile and more adaptable to the new competitive environment. You need to build more resilient workforces with change endurance that can navigate increasing levels of complexity. This includes providing your people leaders with formalized training and support, to help them withstand sustained disruption and navigate change, including ways to focus on creativity and innovation.

There is a great tool the **Change Readiness Assessment** that addresses the seven traits of change readiness. It's a fun and informative team tool to see how your team rates in the seven categories of change readiness. You can use it as a team resource so you know who the go-to person is on your team when you are looking for those that are skilled in resourcefulness, optimism, adventurousness, passion/drive, adaptability, confidence and tolerance for ambiguity.

Change of mindset

Getting people to deal effectively with change demands that they develop a new mindset. In most organizations, doing that requires a very significant transition: old assumptions and expectations have to be relinquished. It isn't enough to preach about the 'Promised Land' or by describing the benefits of continuous improvement or thriving on chaos. It isn't even enough to inspire people with case studies of organizations that are said to be doing these things.

You have to manage the big transition from the old assumptions and expectations of isolated and piecemeal change to the new ones of continuous change. That task is no different from managing any other big transition. Non-stop change is simply a lot of different changes that overlap each other — as changes have always done — as well as an increase in the rate of overlapping change. Every new level of change is termed non-stop by people who are having trouble with transition. This is the reason we started this chapter with the importance of understanding transition and how it differs from change.

The importance of acknowledging endings and dealing with the emotions regarding change, the new beginnings, will ensure the best chance for successfully navigating change in your organization and more specifically with your team. At the same time, every level of change you achieve needs to be viewed or reframed as the new normal. Seen this way, what people today call non-stop change is simply a new level of what has always existed. It's simply their new reality or their new way of being.

These are more than simple arguments about the meanings of words: our perspective, definition and mindset about change make the difference in how we plan, manage and lead successfully through change as leaders.

A practical change management framework

There are many change management frameworks out there and I have read most of them. My favourite is another one of those invaluable tools that came out of my graduate studies, this time my advanced diploma in strategic human resources. It is a model that really resonates with my clients who are people leaders. It's called the **5C Model** and you can find it in ***Change Happens.***

It ties together the essential elements for managing change and does so in a way that makes it easy to understand and apply. The Cs are: communication, confidentiality, cultural compatibility, courtship and completion. Then there are the counter-Cs: concealment, contempt, callous disregard, coercion and confusion which you see when change or transition is stuck.

I think you will like this change model because it is practical and includes templates, processes and tools that you can use right away. Dr. Beth Page was one of my professors at Royal Roads University in B.C., Canada, and the author of *Change Happens.* I have two copies, the signed one she provided after my advanced read of the 2nd edition and a copy that I loan to clients. Once they read it, they buy a copy for themselves and their organization. It's a must-have in your leadership reference books, right alongside this one!

I hope this shift in paradigm, the introduction of transitions, strategies, competency tools and reframing change will allow you to navigate change with confidence and consideration. As people leaders, being aware of and attending to the psychological shifts and related emotions that your people will experience with each change event will serve you well. And it will position you as an agent for change who will thrive in an ever-changing world.

🔍 Reflection Questions

1. **How do I currently perceive and define change — as disruption, opportunity or something else?**

   Reflect on how this mindset influences your reactions and effectiveness in leading your team through change.

   _____
   _____
   _____
   _____
   _____

2. **How am I supporting my team's psychological transition — not just managing change events but attending to their emotional and mental responses?**

   Consider what structures or conversations you facilitate to help people grieve endings and embrace new beginnings.

   _____
   _____
   _____
   _____
   _____

3. **In what ways do I ensure clarity and empowerment around decision-making during periods of change?**

   Think about how well roles, authority, and decision parameters are communicated and whether your team feels enabled to act within those boundaries.

   _____

   _____

   _____

   _____

   _____

4. **How present and attentive am I when engaging with individuals or teams navigating change?**

   Reflect on your ability to listen deeply, notice unspoken concerns and provide the undivided attention needed to build trust and understanding.

   _____

   _____

   _____

   _____

   _____

5. **What strategies am I using to foster change readiness and build resilience within my team or organization?**

   Consider how you are encouraging adaptability, future-focused thinking, and a mindset shift toward continuous change as the new normal.

   _____
   _____
   _____
   _____
   _____

CHAPTER 9

Leading the Feminine-Inspired Way

Through this book, I hope I have convinced you to consider embracing a way of leading in your organizations that emphasizes connection, collaboration and community. This approach, which I call feminine-inspired leadership, has the potential to revolutionize your work environment, your relationship with your employees and your bottom line.

Adapting your leadership style is an ongoing learning journey. I know because I've evolved from that young vocational counsellor to a mature CEO of a global leadership consultancy, and have learned a lot of lessons along the way. Lessons from great leaders, horrible bosses, mentors, team members, our clients and from authors of leadership books like this one. I consider those authors of the books in my learning library as my teachers, and hope that you will see me in the same way.

Although I was fortunate to have many role models who practised non-traditional leadership, in my early career the dominant model was still a masculine paradigm for leadership. It's taken me decades to finetune this feminine-inspired leadership approach. I am grateful to have shared my research, practices, experiences and lessons learned in this book so that you can integrate 'the feminine' into your leadership, right away. I can't guarantee that everything in your team or organization will improve 100 per cent overnight. But if you follow the strategies I have outlined in this book, you will start to see positive results sooner than you thought possible.

This leadership philosophy has been proven to have a profound impact on leaders, teams and organizations. How do I know this? I've been putting this approach into practice into the leadership roles that I have held for over two decades. And because my company, Organizations by Design Inc., has worked with organizations like yours since 2019, and we have been able to help them transform their workplaces into spaces built on a foundation of feminine-inspired leadership, which has had a profound impact on their organizational culture.

Feminine-inspired leadership in practice

To wrap up this book, I thought it would be appropriate to tell the story of one such client, who has fully adopted the feminine-inspired leadership approach. The transformation they have witnessed in themselves as leaders, in their teams and in their organizational culture is nothing short of inspiring.

Let me provide some background. The executive director of an Edmonton child-care and family services agency with more than 60 staff participated in our first online leadership development program called Building Collaborative Learning Teams, along with 64 other leaders from across our province. She was so moved by the transformational experience, powerful content and takeaways, she asked us to come deliver it again to her leadership team. She sat in on the second round to absorb all of the rich content and to learn with her leadership team.

As a result of the impact that second round of training had on transforming their organizational culture, the executive director and her team have continued their engagement with Organizations by Design Inc., inviting us to facilitate an Aligning Our Values session with their entire team and later, our Vision to Impact: A Systems Leadership Journey. The leadership team has also indicated their desire to participate in an upcoming cohort of our Women's Leadership Series.

I tell you this because I'm proud of the work we do at Organizations by Design Inc., and repeat customers are always a good sign. But just as importantly, it's so rewarding when we see our clients experiencing such profound success, having embraced the feminine-inspired leadership philosophy throughout their organization. Their success is our success and tangible evidence of how our approach works.

The executive director was kind enough to allow me to share some of her comments and those of some of her colleagues.

From the executive director:

"This experience impacted me by providing a number of reflective tools (personal values, mental models, awareness wheel) that allowed me to view my leadership through a variety of lenses and to take new perspectives I had not seen before. I will continue to use these tools. The time set aside each week for this learning journey took a level of planning and discipline that I will also bring forward as of high importance in my leadership journey. I am a much more confident leader as a result of this experience. I have built confidence in myself and my skill set. I can clearly see where my strengths are and where the strengths of my team are. I have a clear vision for my leadership and that of the organization. I am excited for the future. I have developed leadership skills holistically: mentally, emotionally, spiritually and strategically. I have a variety of easily accessible tools that allow me to slow down, reflect and plan."

From other members of the team:

"I'm not sure I fully realized some of the challenges I was facing and that there were tools to support me in understanding next steps. By the end of the sessions, I felt much more confident in understanding the position I was in with colleagues. And as a leader, I feel more confident in using different tools to better prepare myself for situations, understand things more deeply and manage interactions in a solution-focused manner. I have a better understanding of who I am in the equation working with others"

"I feel so much better about my current practice, my ability to shift and change when needed, to stay current, to approach/manage challenging situations with confidence and I have a repertoire of resources at my fingertips to refer to when I feel stuck."

"Our leadership team will be a strong collaborative learning team working towards the vision of the organization and this will directly impact the ability of all our teams to become strong collaborative learning teams."

"People are human and not perfect. Teams are made up of individuals who come with their own life experiences that contribute to their own and my own mental models. Being aware of that and reflecting will help with our participation in our learning teams. Being vulnerable to share and uncover it in others will support continued learning."

Truthfully, clients like this, who allow us into their organizations to share our leadership programs, are our greatest teachers. They are working on the front lines daily, and they give us the opportunity to see what their daily reality looks like as leaders in a changing world. They augment our cutting-edge leadership material with something even more valuable — a chance to truly understand the current challenges and what leaders like you are dealing with moment to moment. This in turn ensures that we keep our leadership training real, applicable and meaningful.

If you have been inspired by this book and you want to learn more about how to adapt the feminine-inspired leadership approach in your organization visit us at www.feminineinspiredleadership.ca

Until then, I hope you will keep this book as a go-to reference, and that it will become one of your most valuable resources as you continue to evolve in your leadership.

Thank you for embarking on this journey with me and for allowing me to be a companion on this leg of your leadership journey. I know it's a lot, but just take it one strategy and one day at a time.

You've got this!

APPENDIX A

Resource Toolkits

These are my go-to resources — tested, tried and proven to get results. I share what they are, why they matter and provide a direct link. These tools, strategies, articles and books are integral to the transformative leadership learning experiences we offer our clients. Use them with confidence — they will not steer you wrong.

Chapter 2 Toolkit

Personal Values Assessment

> **What it is:** A self-assessment survey that helps leaders identify their core values and understand their motivations.
>
> **Why it matters:** Clarifying personal values builds authenticity and is foundational to values-driven leadership.
>
> 🔗 Take the Personal Values Assessment (Barrett Values Centre) BVC

* * *

Core Values in the Workplace

> **What it is:** A comprehensive list of 80 personal and professional values to guide workplace behaviour and decisions.
>
> **Why it matters:** Defining and aligning values fosters fit, clarity, engagement and a stronger organizational culture.

🔗 **Where to find it: Values List/Article**
https://www.indeed.com/career-advice/career-development/core-values

* * *

Work Values Inventory Worksheet

What it is: A self-assessment worksheet that will help you to identify those values that you think will be important to you in your work.

Why it matters: The more aligned your work values and your organizational work values are, the better your fit.

🔗 Get the downloadable PDF here Work-values-inventory.pdf

* * *

Make Your Values Mean Something

What it is: A seminal article written by one of my favourite authors: Patrick Lencioni.

Why it matters: Clarity on your personal and organizational values is really at the root of 'good fit'.

🔗 Read the article here Make-Your-Values-Mean-Something.pdf

***

V is for Values

What it is: An article from *The Ready* on making values practical, not just words on a wall.

Why it matters: Clear, lived values guide decisions, build trust, and keep teams aligned. Without them, culture drifts and engagement suffers.

🔗 **Read the article here:** V Is for Values – The Ready
Credit: From *The Ready's Newsletter* at The Ready

Chapter 3-Toolkit

Skills Inventory (Team Competence Mapping)

What it is: A living document where team members list their key skills and change-readiness strengths.

Why it matters: Reinforces trust by making visible who can support what — boosting confidence in each other's capabilities.

🔗 **Download the free template and read the guide here:** https://www.aihr.com/blog/create-skills-matrix-competency-matrix/

* * *

IAP2 Public Participation Spectrum

What it is: A framework outlining five levels of stakeholder engagement — Inform, Consult, Involve, Collaborate, Empower.

Why it matters: Clarifies how stakeholders will participate in decisions, building trust and transparency.

🔗 **Learn more about the International Association for Public Participation IAP2 Spectrum:**
IAP2_Public_Participation_Spectrum.pdf

* * *

Rules of Engagement/Shared Commitments/Boundaries of Action

What it is: A way to identify how you want to work together as a team, or establish a learning environment as a facilitator. It is useful when negotiating expectations, for decision-making and addressing obstacles that come up within teams.

Why it matters: Having a shared understanding of how you want to work together takes the guesswork away, and gives you a set of guidelines that you can refer back to or refresh.

Where to find it: <u>Managing a Team? What are Your Rules of Engagement?</u>

* * *

A Guide to Building Psychological Safety on Your Team

What it is: An article with research-backed guidance on creating an environment where individuals feel safe to speak up, take risks, and express themselves without fear of retribution.

Why it matters: Psychological safety is the foundation of high-performing, trusting, innovative teams. It enables open dialogue, learning from mistakes and diversity of thought.

🔗 **Read the article** from Harvard Business Review: <u>https://hbr.org/2022/12/a-guide-to-building-psychological-safety-on-your-team</u>

Chapter 4–Toolkit

Active Listening

What it is: Overview of what active listening is, its types, and why it's essential.

Why it matters: Improves comprehension, empathy and workplace communication.

🔗 **Read article**: https://www.verywellmind.com/what-is-active-listening-3024343

* * *

Four Communication Styles Quiz

What it is: A model categorizing communication into four main behavioural types.

Why it matters: Helps adapt your style to better connect with others.

🔗 **Learn more**: Communication Styles Quiz: How Do You Communicate?

* * *

16 Personalities Test

What it is: A personality test based on Myers-Briggs theory, adapted into 16 types.

Why it matters: Reveals natural strengths, blind spots and communication preferences.

🔗 **Take the test**: https://www.16personalities.com

Advocacy vs. Inquiry – "Artist's Palette" Model

What it is: A tool for balancing your views (advocacy) with curiosity about others (inquiry).

Why it matters: Prevents one-sided conversations and fosters mutual understanding.

🔗 Learn more: <u>artist's palette balancing advocacy and inquiry visual</u>

* * *

How to Handle Difficult Conversations at Work

What it is: A guide for navigating tense discussions with empathy and clarity.

Why it matters: Provides strategies for managing conflict and finding solutions.

🔗 **Read article:** <u>https://hbr.org/2015/01/how-to-handle-difficult-conversations-at-work</u>

Chapter 5 –Toolkit

Growth Mindset vs Fixed Mindset

What it is: A concept popularized by psychologist Dr. Carol Dweck that contrasts two core beliefs about ability: a *fixed mindset* (believing abilities are static) and a *growth mindset* (believing abilities can be developed through effort, strategies and feedback).

Why it matters: Leaders with a growth mindset are more adaptable, resilient and open to learning — qualities essential for navigating change and inspiring high-performing teams. Cultivating a growth mindset encourages continuous improvement and innovation.

Where to find it: URL: https://online.hbs.edu/blog/post/growth-mindset-vs-fixed-mindset

* * *

What Having a Growth Mindset Actually Means

What it is: An article exploring what having a "growth mindset" truly means—the belief that intelligence and abilities can be developed through dedication, effort, feedback, and learning. It contrasts with a "fixed mindset," where talents are seen as static and unchangeable.

Why it matters: Embracing a growth mindset fosters resilience, motivation, adaptability, and continuous progress. It transforms challenges into learning opportunities rather than threats.

Where to find it: *Harvard Business Review* What Having a "Growth Mindset" Actually Means

* * *

The Fifth Discipline: The Art & Practice of the Learning Organization

What it is: A seminal work introducing five disciplines (including systems thinking and personal mastery) that define a learning organization.

Why it matters: It offers foundational concepts for building organizations that continually learn and adapt collectively.

Where to find it: <u>the fifth discipline</u>

* * *

Humble Inquiry: The Gentle Art of Asking Instead of Telling

What it is: A resource about a communication approach advocating for curiosity-based questions rather than directive statements to engage others.

Why it matters: Encourages trust, openness and more meaningful collaboration by acknowledging others' knowledge and perspectives.

Where to find it:
https://www.15minutebusinessbooks.com/blog/2021/08/11/humble-inquiry-the-gentle-art-of-asking-instead-of-telling-second-edition-by-edgar-schein-and-peter-schein-here-are-my-five-lessons-and-takeaways/

* * *

After-Action Review (AAR)

What it is: A rapid debrief method asking what was intended, what happened, why gaps occurred and what to improve next time.

Why it matters: It accelerates learning by capturing insights immediately after actions and feeding them into future improvements.

Where to find it: https://commonslibrary.org/before-action-reviews-bars-and-after-action-reviews-aars/

* * *

The Systems Iceberg Model

What it is: A visual tool for exploring underlying patterns, structures and mental models beneath observable events.

Why it matters: Helps leaders see beyond surface issues to address root causes and drive meaningful organizational change.

Where to find it: https://untools.co/iceberg-model/

* * *

Building a Learning Organization

What it is: A *Harvard Business Review* article laying out the principles and practices of creating organizations that learn.

Why it matters: Offers a proven framework for leaders seeking to evolve culture and systems toward continuous improvement.

Where to find it: https://hbr.org/1993/07/building-a-learning-organization

Chapter 6 Tool Kit

SWOT Analysis

What it is: A strategic tool that maps strengths, weaknesses, opportunities and threats to evaluate internal capabilities and external possibilities.

Why it matters: It offers a clear framework for organizations to align their strengths with opportunities while addressing risks and gaps in planning.

Where to find it:
https://www.investopedia.com/terms/s/swot.asp

* * *

PESTLE Analysis

What it is: A framework that examines political, economic, social, technological, legal and environmental factors shaping the external environment.

Why it matters: By tracking these macro-environmental influences, organizations can anticipate and respond strategically to external changes.

Where to find it: https://onstrategyhq.com/resources/pestle-analysis/

* * *

Systems Thinking Tools

What it is: One of the best places to find resources on systems thinking like the **Habits of a Systems Thinker** habits-single-page-2020 and Tools Studio.

Why it matters: Applying these tools helps leaders see patterns and interconnections, enabling them to act on root causes rather than symptoms.

Where to find it: Waters Centre for Systems Thinking: https://waterscenterst.org/

* * *

Mental Models Mapping

What it is: A technique that visualizes hidden assumptions and beliefs shaping how we interpret situations.

Why it matters: Surfacing these mental models increases self-awareness and enables more adaptive and informed decision-making.

Where to find it: https://www.habitsforthinking.in/article/a-comprehensive-guide-to-mental-models batonglobal.com

* * *

Ladder of Inference

What it is: A conceptual model by Dr. Chris Argyris illustrating how observations are filtered through assumptions to drive quick judgments and actions.

Why it matters: It helps teams pause, surface assumptions and ensure decisions are grounded in clarity rather than reactivity.

Where to find it: https://www.toolshero.com/decision-making/ladder-of-inference/

Building Self-Awareness to Be A Better Human-Centered Leader - Harvard Business Impact

Chapter 7 Toolkit

Myers–Briggs Type Indicator (MBTI)

What it is: A personality assessment identifying preferences in perception and decision-making across 16 types.

Why it matters: Improves self-awareness, communication and collaboration by understanding diverse personality patterns.

🔗 **Learn more:** https://www.myersbriggs.org/my-mbti-personality-type/mbti-basics/

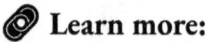

Team Dynamics | Visualize Team Personality Insights

What it is: A tool for mapping and visualizing team members' personality traits, preferences and working styles.

Why it matters: Helps leaders align strengths, anticipate challenges and build cohesive, high-performing teams.

🔗 **Learn more:** https://www.psychometrics.com/assessments/team-dynamics/

* * *

Creating Connections: How Friendships Feed the Soul

What it is: An anthology co-authored by Nicole van Kuppeveld (that's me) and 21 inspiring storytellers that delves into how deep, authentic friendships enrich emotional well-being, resilience and personal connection.

Why it matters: Cultivating meaningful relationships supports mental and emotional health — necessary ingredients for grounded, empathetic leadership and strong team culture.

Where to find it: https://www.amazon.ca/s?k=Creating+Connections%3A+How+Friendships+Feed+the+Soul

* * *

Emotional Intelligence Tests

What it is: 17 assessments measuring your ability to recognize, understand and manage emotions — both your own and others'.

Why it matters: Boosts communication, strengthens relationships and helps leaders handle conflict, motivate teams and create psychological safety.

🔗 **Learn more:** Emotional Intelligence Test / Quiz | Psychology Today

* * *

Thomas–Kilmann Conflict Mode Instrument (TKI)

What it is: A self-assessment identifying preferred conflict-handling styles — collaborating, accommodating, competing, avoiding or compromising.

Why it matters: Builds conflict awareness and equips leaders to resolve issues constructively.

🔗 **Learn more:** https://kilmanndiagnostics.com/overview-thomas-kilmann-conflict-mode-instrument-tki/

* * *

DISC Assessment

What it is: A personality assessment revealing communication and behavioural styles — dominance, influence, steadiness and conscientiousness.

Why it matters: Enhances collaboration by helping leaders adapt to diverse communication preferences.

🔗 **Learn more:** https://www.discprofile.com/

Chapter 8 Toolkit

William Bridges' Model of Transition

What it is: A framework that distinguishes between change (external events) and transition (internal process) with three phases—ending, neutral zone and new beginning.

Why it matters: Helps leaders guide people through the emotional and psychological side of change for smoother adoption of the new normal.

Where to find it: https://wmbridges.com/about/what-is-transition/

* * *

Facilitator's Guide to Participatory Decision-Making

What it is: A practical manual for designing and leading collaborative decision-making processes by Dr. Sam Kaner.

Why it matters: Builds inclusive engagement, ensures diverse input and strengthens group ownership of outcomes.

Where to find it: https://www.amazon.com/Facilitators-Guide-Participatory-Decision-Making/dp/1118404955

* * *

Change Readiness Assessment

What it is: A diagnostic tool that evaluates an organization's preparedness for change, including culture, leadership and resources.

Why it matters: Identifies strengths and gaps to address before implementing change, improving success rates.

Where to find it: 2_-change_readiness_assessment_0426111.pdf

* * *

Change Happens + 5C Model

What it is: A five-step change framework—clarity, communication, connection, capability and capacity — created by change leadership expert Dr. Beth Page.

Why it matters: Provides a structured approach to engage people and resources effectively during organizational change.

Where to find it: Amazon.ca : change happens

APPENDIX B

Feminine-Inspired Case Studies & Stories

These AI-generated case studies and stories were created using the book's rich content to bring each chapter's concepts to life. Each one walks you through a realistic leadership scenario, showing how you might approach the challenge using the tools and strategies in the chapter. They offer a clear, relatable path you can adapt to your own context — no matter your sector. Note: None of these are real companies.

- Clarifying Values for Organizational Success at Stratwell Partners (Professional Services)
- Rebuilding Trust at ThriveTech (Tech)
- The Power of Communication in Leadership – A Journey at Bright Futures Alliance (Not for Profit)
- Phoenix Manufacturing: A Struggling Organization (Manufacturing)
- The Thinking Shift — How One Non-profit Leader Transformed Her Organization by Creating Thinking Spaces (Nonprofit)
- Real World Stories
    a. Apple's Health App – No Women on the Team
    b. Kodak's Missed Digital Future – Echo Chamber Thinking
    c. LEGO Rebuilds with Girls in Mind – Co-Design & Inclusion

d. Microsoft's Inclusive Design Lab – Disability as a Source of Innovation
  e. NASA and the Challenger Disaster—A Tragic Lesson in Groupthink
- The Power of Relationship-Building in Leadership (Tech)
- Leading Through Storm at Meridian Health Group (Healthcare)

Clarifying Values for Organizational Success at Stratwell Partners (Professional Services)

Background

Stratwell Partners is a national consulting firm specializing in strategy, operations, and change management for mid-to-large organizations. Recently, the firm secured a high-profile engagement with a multinational retail chain to redesign their supply chain operations. This was a complex, time-sensitive project involving multiple internal teams, the client's executive leadership and several external vendors.

The leadership team at Stratwell knew the technical expertise was there—but without strong alignment around shared values, the firm risked falling into siloed work, inconsistent decision-making and strained client relationships. Unfortunately, the company's stated values were vague and inconsistently applied, leading to communication breakdowns and differing interpretations of "how we work together."

The Challenge

Without a clearly defined and operationalized set of values, Stratwell Partners faced several issues:

- Lack of Transparency: Project teams were unclear on priorities, creating delays and duplicated work.
- Client Misalignment: The retail client wasn't sure where Stratwell stood on certain principles, leading to misunderstandings about deliverables and decision-making authority.
- Staff Turnover: A few high-performing consultants left, citing cultural misalignment.

- Inconsistent Decision-Making: Leaders handled similar situations differently, creating confusion and eroding trust.

The Turning Point

Recognizing the cultural drift, Stratwell's managing partners engaged a leadership consultant to facilitate a values-alignment process. The aim was to clearly define the firm's values, embed them into day-to-day operations, and ensure every team member understood how to apply them in client work.

The consultant introduced a Values Inventory, enabling employees to compare personal values with the firm's stated ones. This revealed significant gaps between what was written on paper and what was experienced in practice, sparking meaningful conversations about alignment and behaviour.

The Process

1. **Values Assessment**
   Partners and senior managers completed the Barrett Values Inventory, then shared personal and organizational value reflections in a facilitated session.

2. **Defining Organizational Values**
   The team refined their core values — integrity, collaboration, and client impact — translating them into specific behaviours and decision-making criteria for consulting work.

3. **Transparency and Openness**
   Leadership committed to openly sharing project priorities, challenges and decision rationales, ensuring alignment both internally and with clients.

4. **Aligning Behaviour with Values**
   Expectations were set for living the values in every client engagement, from how feedback was delivered to how cross-functional teams collaborated.

The Outcome

- **Increased Trust:** Consultants felt more connected to leadership decisions, fostering stronger team cohesion.
- **Better Collaboration:** Transparency and shared principles improved co-ordination between service lines.
- **Stronger Culture:** Employees began actively practising the firm's values, increasing engagement and retention.
- **Successful Client Delivery:** The supply chain redesign was completed ahead of schedule, earning high praise from the retail client.

Why Professional Service Firms Need Values Alignment

The Stratwell Partners example illustrates how service-based firms — where relationships, trust, and reputation are everything—cannot afford to let values sit as abstract statements. A skilled facilitator can:

- Bring Expertise to guide complex, candid discussions.
- Use Proven Tools to make values tangible and measurable.
- Offer Neutral Insight to identify cultural blind spots.
- Create Real Outcomes by embedding values into client-facing work.
- Ensure Long-Term Cultural Health by making values part of every-day decisions.

Reflection for Leaders

- Do your values guide your decisions when client pressures rise?

- Can your team clearly articulate what your values mean in practice?
- Are you confident that your culture reflects your stated values?

Stratwell Partners discovered that defining and operationalizing values was not just a cultural exercise — it was a competitive advantage.

Rebuilding Trust at ThriveTech (Tech)

Background

ThriveTech, a mid-sized technology company specializing in software solutions for the health-care industry, faced a critical challenge: a trust deficit within its product development team. Known for its innovative products, the company's latest project — a cutting-edge patient management system — was faltering. Internal discord, marked by poor collaboration, eroding morale, and missed deadlines, threatened to derail the company's reputation and financial stability.

The product development team was a diverse group of senior engineers, junior developers and project managers. While technically skilled, they struggled with interpersonal dynamics. Conflicts over project timelines, perceived inequities, and lack of transparency in decision-making created a toxic environment. Trust, the bedrock of successful collaboration, was conspicuously absent.

The Crisis of Trust: ThriveTech's trust issues manifested in several ways:
Doubt in Competence: Team members second-guessed each other's expertise, leading to micromanagement and inefficiency.
Unmet Commitments: Deadlines were routinely missed, eroding confidence in reliability.
Psychological Insecurity: Fear of judgment silenced innovative ideas and honest feedback.

Fragmented Communication: Silos formed as individuals avoided collaboration, undermining the project's cohesion.

The executive team realized the stakes: without intervention, the project would fail, and the organization's broader culture might suffer irreparable damage.

Turning to Leadership Expertise: Recognizing the complexity of rebuilding trust, ThriveTech's Chief Technology Officer (CTO) engaged a professional leadership coach. The coach's expertise in trust-building was pivotal in addressing the root causes of dysfunction. They proposed a tailored approach based on the six dimensions of trust: competence, reliability, integrity, vulnerability, intentionality and emotional connection.

The Intervention: The leadership coach initiated a structured process, beginning with a two-day workshop to address the team's trust challenges. And then:

1. Conducted a skill-mapping exercise to highlight and validate individual strengths.
2. Introduced peer mentoring to foster mutual respect and understanding of capabilities.
3. Created a shared accountability framework with clearly defined roles and deliverables.
4. Instituted weekly progress meetings to ensure transparency and alignment.
5. Facilitated the development of a team charter emphasizing honesty and fairness.
6. Encouraged leadership to model ethical behaviour by openly acknowledging past missteps.
7. Provided a safe platform for team members to share challenges and aspirations.
8. Organized team-building activities to humanize relationships and build empathy.
9. Conducted visioning exercises to unify the team around shared goals and values.
10. Communicated the broader purpose of the project to deepen commitment.

11. Delivered training in active listening and emotional intelligence.
12. Celebrated milestones and individual contributions to foster a culture of appreciation.

Results: Within months, ThriveTech's product development team exhibited a remarkable transformation:

Improved Collaboration: Members worked cohesively, leveraging each other's strengths.

Reliable Performance: Commitments were met consistently, reducing project delays.

Enhanced Innovation: Restored psychological safety led to bold ideas and breakthroughs.

Boosted Morale: Trust and mutual respect created a positive, engaged work environment.

The patient management system was delivered on the revised timeline, earning industry acclaim and solidifying ThriveTech's reputation as a leader in healthcare technology.

Lessons for Leaders: ThriveTech's journey highlights the profound impact of trust — or its absence — on team performance and organizational outcomes. Leaders who proactively cultivate trust unlock unparalleled potential for collaboration, innovation and resilience.

Building trust is a nuanced and ongoing process requiring specialized skills and frameworks.

For success you need:
Objective Analysis: Identifying root causes of trust issues.
Tailored Solutions: Designing interventions suited to the organization's unique context.

Sustained Growth: Empowering teams with tools to maintain and deepen trust over time.

Reflection for Leaders:
Are trust gaps holding your team back?
How can you integrate trust-building practices into your leadership style?
Would partnering with a leadership expert accelerate your team's success?

Trust is not just a virtue; it is a strategic advantage. Leaders who invest in building trust pave the way for lasting organizational success.

The Power of Communication in Leadership – A Journey at Bright Futures Alliance

Background

Bright Futures Alliance is a non-profit dedicated to empowering individuals in vulnerable situations to build safer, more hopeful lives. Its team of deeply committed professionals works in a fast-paced, emotionally demanding environment where stakes are high and challenges are complex. Despite their passion and dedication, the leadership team faced persistent communication challenges — unclear vision, tense team dynamics and difficulty navigating crucial conversations.

The Challenge

The leadership group at Bright Futures Alliance was navigating a period of change, including shifts in roles and responsibilities. This created uncertainty, stress and friction across the team. Team members often expressed that they didn't feel fully heard, and some lacked confidence to speak up in critical moments. Without a shared understanding of organizational goals, mixed messages and conflicting priorities emerged.

At the heart of the issue was a gap in advanced communication skills. Without the tools or confidence to address these challenges directly, misunderstandings multiplied, morale dipped, and performance suffered.

The Solution

Recognizing that strong communication is the foundation of effective leadership, Bright Futures Alliance partnered with us to strengthen their leaders' ability to navigate tough conversations and create clarity within their teams. A customized leadership development program was designed with three key priorities: building confidence, developing active listening and creating shared agreements for communication.

Key Interventions

1. **Building Confidence in Communication**
   Leaders were guided to move beyond simply giving instructions, focusing instead on creating meaningful connections, building trust and understanding diverse perspectives. Through role-play scenarios, they practised tackling challenging issues, delivering direct feedback, and preparing for high-stakes discussions — all in a safe learning space.

2. **Active Listening and Shared Language**
   Leaders explored active listening as more than hearing words — it became about truly understanding the emotions and intentions behind them. One powerful exercise involved repeating back what they had heard and confirming accuracy before responding, helping leaders catch misunderstandings before they escalated.

3. **Shared Commitments and Rules of Engagement**
   The team co-created "Rules of Engagement" — clear agreements on how they would communicate, handle conflict and make decisions. These shared commitments established accountability, ensuring communication remained respectful, transparent and consistent.

4. **Navigating Crucial Conversations**
   Using a structured framework, leaders learned to approach high-stakes, emotionally charged conversations with preparation and presence. Instead of avoiding these discussions, they began to see them as opportunities to align, solve problems and build trust.

The Outcome

- **Clarity and Trust**: Leaders could now clearly articulate the organization's vision, boosting morale and reducing confusion.

- **Improved Relationships**: Respectful, confident communication strengthened bonds within the team, helping resolve issues before they grew.
- **Enhanced Collaboration**: Active listening and shared language led to more unified decision-making and less siloed work.
- **A Culture of Learning**: Leaders embraced difficult conversations as part of growth, fostering a culture where challenges were met with openness instead of avoidance.

Reflection

The Bright Futures Alliance case study shows how communication gaps can hold even the most committed leaders back. When leaders lack the skills to express themselves clearly, listen deeply and address conflict directly, team alignment and morale suffer.

But when leaders actively invest in their communication skills — particularly for crucial conversations — they create the conditions for trust, collaboration and a workplace where every voice matters.

Key Takeaways for Leaders

- Communication is more than information — it's connection, trust and shared understanding.
- Crucial conversations are growth opportunities, not roadblocks.
- Active listening builds stronger relationships and prevents misunderstandings.
- Shared commitments provide a foundation for clarity and accountability.
- Consistent, clear communication keeps teams aligned and focused.

Phoenix Manufacturing: A Struggling Organization (Manufacturing)

Company Background

Phoenix Manufacturing, a family-owned company producing industrial equipment, has operated for over 40 years. Known for its sturdy products, Phoenix maintained steady sales in its early years. However, the past decade has been marked by stagnation in growth and innovation. New competitors with modern technologies have steadily eroded Phoenix's market share.

The company operates with rigid hierarchies and a culture where seniority often outweighs fresh ideas. Leadership emphasizes maintaining traditions and proven methods rather than exploring new approaches. Although the leadership team recognizes challenges, their solutions tend to focus on short-term fixes rather than systemic improvements.

Challenges of a Non-Learning Organization

1. Resistance to Change

Phoenix's leadership clings to its long-standing methods, dismissing employee suggestions for process improvements as too risky or unnecessary. This resistance discourages innovation and adaptability.

- **Impact**: The company lags in adopting newer, more efficient manufacturing technologies, leading to higher production costs and lower efficiency than competitors.

2. Lack of Knowledge Sharing

The siloed structure of Phoenix prevents cross-departmental collaboration. Teams rarely communicate lessons learned from successful or failed projects, leaving no mechanism to leverage collective insights.

- **Impact**: Repeated errors occur across projects, with no framework to capture and share solutions organization-wide.

3. Deficient Feedback Mechanisms

Employees hesitate to provide honest feedback due to a fear of reprisal or being ignored. Leaders rarely seek input from frontline staff, believing they lack the perspective needed for strategic decisions.

- **Impact**: Valuable insights are lost, and problems that could be addressed early are allowed to escalate.

4. Narrow Focus on Outcomes

Phoenix prioritizes short-term profits over long-term growth. This focus discourages experimentation, as any failure is seen as a waste of resources rather than a learning opportunity.

- **Impact**: The company struggles to innovate, and morale among employees plummets as they feel undervalued and constrained.

5. Absence of Psychological Safety

The punitive culture at Phoenix stifles creativity and critical thinking. Employees avoid proposing ideas or taking calculated risks, fearing personal blame if something goes wrong.

- **Impact**: The organization misses opportunities for growth and problem-solving, further entrenching its outdated methods.

The Transformation: To Becoming a Learning Organization

Step 1: Foster a Learning Culture

Phoenix must prioritize cultivating a culture where learning is celebrated and individuals feel empowered to explore and share ideas.

- **Psychological Safety**: Create an environment where employees feel safe to speak openly and share diverse perspectives without fear of judgment or reprisal.
- **Recognition**: Celebrate not just successes but also well-intentioned failures that lead to valuable insights.

Step 2: Implement a Learning Framework

Introduce structured methods for fostering individual, team and organizational learning:

1. **After-Action Reviews**: Conduct reviews after every major project to document lessons learned and share them across teams.
2. **Start, Stop, Continue**: Regularly assess what practices should be adopted, abandoned or improved organization-wide.
3. **Knowledge Sharing Platforms**: Establish systems for documenting and disseminating insights, such as an internal wiki or collaborative tools.

Step 3: Embrace Systems Thinking

Train leadership and teams to view the organization as a set of interconnected systems. Encourage exploring how decisions in one area impact others, promoting more thoughtful and strategic actions.

- **Example**: Analyzing how delays in procurement affect production timelines and customer satisfaction, then finding systemic solutions rather than placing blame on a single department.

Step 4: Build Team and Organizational Learning

- **Team Learning**: Facilitate workshops, cross-departmental meetings and brainstorming sessions to encourage collaboration and leverage diverse perspectives.
- **Organizational Learning**: Invest in leadership development programs that emphasize adaptability and systems thinking.

Step 5: Embed Continuous Feedback and Evaluation

- **Regular Feedback Loops**: Establish channels for two-way feedback between employees and leadership.
- **Evaluation Mechanisms**: Use tools like surveys and performance metrics to assess the effectiveness of learning initiatives, adapting as needed.

Step 6: Integrate Coaching and a Coaching Approach

Equip leaders with coaching skills to empower their teams, encourage reflection and foster growth. By shifting from a directive leadership style to one that asks thoughtful questions, Phoenix can unlock employee potential.

Potential Outcomes of the Transformation

By adopting the principles of a learning organization, Phoenix can expect:

- **Improved Innovation**: A culture that values learning and experimentation will result in more creative solutions and product offerings.
- **Higher Engagement**: Employees will feel valued, increasing motivation, retention and collaboration.

- **Enhanced Efficiency**: Sharing knowledge and integrating systems thinking will streamline processes and reduce redundancies.
- **Market Competitiveness**: With a more adaptive and innovative culture, Phoenix will regain its edge over competitors.

Conclusion

Phoenix Manufacturing's transformation from a rigid, non-learning organization to a dynamic learning organization hinges on its commitment to cultural change. By fostering a learning environment rooted in trust, defined rules of engagement, leveraging diversity and systems thinking, Phoenix can adapt to the evolving business landscape, enabling it to thrive for decades to come.

The Thinking Shift — How One Non-profit Leader Transformed Her Organization by Creating Thinking Spaces (Non-profit)

Organization: *HopeBridge* – A non-profit focused on youth mental health in underserved communities across Western Canada.

Leader: *Sasha*, Executive Director

* * *

When Sasha stepped into the Executive Director role at HopeBridge, she brought with her a deep passion for youth mental health and a reputation for getting things done. Under her leadership, the organization had grown significantly — tripling its reach within two years, winning new grants, and expanding into new regions. On paper, everything looked like success.

But internally, Sasha was burning out.

In a leadership development sessions, Sasha confessed something that felt counter to her image of strong leadership:

> "I'm in back-to-back meetings all day, answering emails late into the night, and somehow I still feel like I'm falling behind. I'm doing everything... except thinking clearly."

This statement became a pivotal moment in our work together.

The Challenge: Drowning in Activity, Starved for Strategy

Like many non-profit leaders, Sasha wore many hats — overseeing fundraising, managing a growing team, representing the organization in community partnerships, and responding to urgent client needs. Her calendar reflected her commitment. But it also reflected a trap.

She had fallen into what we call *the busy leader loop*: constantly responding to urgent issues, making rapid decisions without reflection, and reacting rather than anticipating.

During her strategic leadership coaching session, it became clear that Sasha was struggling with the same issue many high-performing leaders face: the absence of structured time for thinking. Her leadership was strong—but it lacked the space to stretch, evolve and lead with vision.

The consequences were beginning to show:

- A quick hiring decision created division within a newly formed program team.
- Staff felt overworked and unclear about shifting priorities.
- Stakeholder relationships were starting to feel transactional rather than strategic.
- Sasha herself described feeling like "a firefighter, not a leader."

The Intervention: Two Hours to Think

Sasha was challenged to make one high-leverage shift: **block two hours a week for intentional thinking**. No emails. No meetings. No distractions. Just time to reflect, map, and process.

This wasn't time off—it was time *on purpose*.

This paired this with targeted leadership development work in three key areas:

1. **Strategic Thinking:**
    Sasha explored tools like SWOT, PESTLE, and root-cause analysis not as templates to fill out, but as frameworks to slow down and structure her thinking. Together, we identified where her strategy was being drowned out by immediacy—and how she could reclaim control of her agenda.

2. **Systems Thinking:**
   Through visual mapping exercises, she zoomed out to look at the broader ecosystem in which HopeBridge operated. We used systems thinking to uncover how small changes — like shifting how they onboard new partners — could have a ripple effect across program outcomes, fundraising, and team morale.

3. **Mental Models and Adaptive Thinking:**
   Sasha had internalized the belief that "leaders should always be available." This was driving her toward over-functioning and robbing her team of opportunities to grow. In our sessions, we unpacked that belief — exploring its roots and challenging its usefulness. We reframed her leadership identity to include space for reflection, learning, and deliberate decision-making.

She also began to recognize her own cognitive filters — how assumptions shaped her communication with the board, and how past experiences were influencing how she interpreted staff behaviour. Through tools like the **Ladder of Inference**, Sasha began slowing down the process of how she formed conclusions and responded to situations, opening up space for inquiry and connection.

The Transformation: From Firefighting to Future-Shaping

A month after committing to her "thinking time," Sasha returned to her session noticeably different. There was more clarity in her tone. More pause. More purpose.

> "Those two hours saved me ten," she said. "I used to just react. Now, I ask better questions, make clearer decisions, and delegate more confidently. I'm finally leading again."

Here's what changed at HopeBridge:

Sharper Decision-Making

Sasha paused a proposed expansion plan that, upon reflection, would have stretched their capacity and diluted their impact. Instead, she focused on consolidating and strengthening current programs — an unpopular decision at first, but one that stabilized the team and improved client outcomes.

Stronger Communication

She implemented "clarity check-ins" in team meetings — creating intentional space to align understanding, check assumptions and surface hidden tensions. Staff reported feeling more heard and more clear.

Empowered Team Culture

By moving away from over-functioning and toward *coaching her team*, Sasha allowed her staff to think for themselves. This shift created a culture of ownership and critical thinking, rather than one of dependency.

Renewed Vision and Strategic Alignment

With space to think, Sasha began reconnecting to the vision of the organization. In a strategic retreat with her board — designed and facilitated through a feminine-informed appreciative inquiry approach — we used the 5-D process (Define, Discover, Dream, Design, Destiny) to surface strategic directives that were not only clear and energizing but co-owned by the board. Note: This is the appreciative inquiry framework.

Psychological Safety and Diversity of Thought

Sasha leaned into the discomfort of being challenged. She started inviting diverse perspectives into leadership conversations, including those that contradicted her own. As one staff member shared anonymously in a feedback survey:

"It feels like we're finally allowed to think differently, not just execute."

***

Lessons Learned: Leadership Thinking as a Practice, Not an Accident

Sasha's transformation wasn't just personal — it was cultural and organizational. By investing in her own development, she gave permission for her team to do the same. She proved what research and experience both show: **the quality of a leader's thinking has a direct impact on their decisions, their communication, their culture and their outcomes.**

Here are a few best practices that emerged from her case:

- **Thinking time is not optional for effective leadership.** It's a discipline that needs to be protected and prioritized. Even two hours a week can radically shift a leader's perspective and effectiveness.
- **High-quality thinking requires intentional tools.** Sasha didn't just sit in silence — she used visual mapping, strategic frameworks and systems thinking to structure her reflections and make connections.
- **Leadership development accelerates this shift.** Without guided coaching, structured inquiry, and reflective practice, it's too easy for leaders to default to habits of reactivity and busyness.
- **Mental models matter.** Challenging her internal assumptions about what leadership should look like gave Sasha the freedom to show up differently — for herself and her team.

- **Culture follows thinking.** When leaders model curiosity, intentionality and strategic reflection, it creates permission for others to do the same.

The Takeaway: Thinking is the Work

HopeBridge's story is more than a tale of one leader finding balance. It's a real-world example of what happens when leadership thinking becomes a daily practice — not an afterthought.

Sasha didn't need a new CRM, a bigger board, or another strategic plan. She needed time, tools and support to think. That investment created a ripple effect through every part of her organization — from staff culture to board alignment to program impact.

In a world that moves fast, it's easy to equate movement with progress. But effective leadership isn't just about doing more. It's about thinking better.

Real World Stories Section

Here are five short stories—two showing failures due to lack of diversity and two showing successes due to inclusive perspectives. The fifth highlights the value of diversity of thought and how one different perspective prevented costly groupthink. Note: All AI generated, but based on real companies that learned and shared their lessons learned.

* * *

▼ **Failure**

Apple's Health App — No Women on the Team (2014)

What happened:
Apple launched its iOS Health app as a comprehensive wellness tracker. It tracked everything from blood pressure to steps... but completely left out menstrual cycle tracking — something critical to half the population.

Why it failed:
Despite being marketed as a "complete" health tracker, there were no women in decision-making roles on the app team. This blind spot not only hurt credibility but also alienated a large user base.

Lesson:
When teams lack gender diversity, they miss key use cases. Inclusion = better product design.

* * *

▼ Failure

Kodak's Missed Digital Future Echo Chamber Thinking

What happened:
Kodak actually invented the first digital camera in 1975. But senior leadership, dominated by traditionalists, dismissed the idea. They feared it would cannibalize their film business.

Why it failed:
With no internal culture of dissent or cross-generational voices, Kodak clung to a legacy model while competitors like Sony and Canon surged ahead in digital.

Lesson:
Without diverse thinking and voices willing to challenge assumptions, innovation stalls — and giants fall.

* * *

☑ Success

LEGO Rebuilds with Girls in Mind (2012+) –Co-Design & Inclusion

What happened:
LEGO saw a major gender gap in its user base—only nine per cent of their users were girls. Instead of guessing, they launched a four-year study, partnering with psychologists, parents, and kids to understand what girls wanted.

Why it worked:
They co-designed new product lines like LEGO Friends, adding story-driven sets and more diverse characters. It paid off: the brand saw a double-digit boost in female engagement and billions in new revenue.

Lesson:
Inviting diverse users into the process isn't just ethical — it's profitable.

* * *

☑ Success

Microsoft's Inclusive Design Lab –Disability as a Source of Innovation

What happened:
Microsoft created an Inclusive Design Lab focused on people with disabilities — not as a "niche," but as a source of breakthrough solutions.

Result:
The Xbox Adaptive Controller was born. Designed with input from gamers with mobility challenges, it became not just a tool for inclusion but also a brand differentiator and a viral success story.

Lesson:
When you build *with* marginalized voices, not just *for* them, you unlock innovation for everyone.

* * *

☑ Success

NASA and the Challenger Disaster—A Tragic Lesson in Groupthink (And a Success That Followed)

What happened:
In 1986, the Challenger space shuttle exploded, killing all seven astronauts on board. A later investigation revealed that engineers had warned against launching in cold temperatures, fearing O-ring failure.

But NASA leaders, under immense pressure to stick to timelines, dismissed dissenting voices. There was a culture of consensus and optimism — *groupthink* — that overrode caution.

The shift:

After the disaster, NASA made major organizational changes, embedding dissent protocols and red-teaming — essentially assigning someone to challenge assumptions and decisions, no matter how unpopular.

Later, during the Mars Pathfinder mission (1997), this approach paid off. A newly formed diverse mission team, including young engineers, women and people outside the traditional aerospace mold, flagged key risks in testing that could've resulted in a failure. Because open disagreement was now welcomed, the team adjusted course — and landed safely.

Lesson:

Diversity of thought isn't just about demographics — it's about psychological safety and empowering people to challenge the majority view. In high-stakes environments, that one divergent perspective can literally save lives.

Case Study: The Power of Relationship-Building in Leadership

Background

At a mid-sized tech company, TechVision, things had been moving fast. The team — comprising engineers, designers and product managers — was highly skilled, with each member contributing deep technical expertise to the company's success. However, as the company grew, something started to shift. While the team was producing high-quality work, there was an undercurrent of disconnection that couldn't be ignored. Employees worked in silos, communication was strained, and morale was beginning to dip. Even though the team was talented, the lack of collaboration and trust was starting to take a toll.

Leadership recognized the challenge: How could they turn around the team dynamic, foster more authentic relationships, and cultivate a culture of trust and collaboration? They knew that making these changes wasn't just about adjusting processes — it required shifting how people connected with each other on a personal and professional level.

The Challenge

Despite the technical prowess of the team, something was missing — a sense of connection. There was little trust between team members, and many operated as though they were working in isolation. Conversations often felt transactional and feedback was rare. Meanwhile, a hierarchical structure had created a subtle divide between staff and leadership, fueling an "us vs. them" mentality. This fragmentation made it harder for people to communicate openly, collaborate on innovative solutions and address challenges as a unified team.

The leadership team recognized that while they had the talent and capability to solve these issues, they needed a way to create stronger relationships — both within the team and across the organization — that could lead to better communication, more creative problem-solving, and a greater sense of ownership and satisfaction.

A Shift in Focus: Building Authentic Relationships

In order to improve things, leadership began to focus on relationship-building, recognizing that authentic connections would be the foundation for a more collaborative, high-performing team.

They started by prioritizing one-on-one conversations with team members, not just to discuss work but to get to know them as people. Through these discussions, they learned about each team member's passions, motivations and career goals. More importantly, they also identified the challenges their people were facing: communication bottlenecks, lack of support in cross-department collaboration, and feeling disconnected from the leadership team.

One particular challenge stood out: two senior engineers, Alice and Peter, had worked together at a previous company and had a strong friendship that occasionally influenced how they interacted with others. Leadership didn't ignore the dynamic but instead took the opportunity to address it directly — acknowledging the friendship while stressing the importance of transparency and open communication within the team. This helped prevent potential friction and laid the groundwork for a more inclusive environment.

Creating an Open and Safe Environment

Alongside one-on-one meetings, leadership began encouraging a culture of transparency and psychological safety. They knew that building trust required not only listening but creating a space where team members felt comfortable taking risks and speaking up.

For example, in team meetings, leadership began introducing open-ended questions designed to foster deeper dialogue. Instead of jumping straight into the business at hand, they'd ask questions like, "What's a challenge you're currently facing, in this team or with other stakeholders?" This simple shift in approach encouraged team members to open up, share their concerns, and express their unique perspectives. It wasn't about just solving problems — it was about building understanding and empathy.

As a result, team members started to open up more, offering ideas and feedback more freely. They felt safer sharing their challenges, knowing that leadership was actively creating an environment where vulnerability was welcomed.

Connecting Beyond Work

Realizing that authentic relationships don't just form during formal meetings, leadership also began organizing informal events to build connections beyond the office. Monthly "Lunch & Learn" sessions were introduced, where team members could share their personal interests or talk about experiences outside of work. These events not only allowed employees to get to know each other better but also helped to break down the professional barriers that often kept people in silos.

These efforts fostered a deeper sense of camaraderie, helping employees realize that they weren't just colleagues but individuals with diverse passions and backgrounds. As they grew closer, the team began to collaborate more effectively, exchanging ideas and supporting each other in ways they hadn't before.

Overcoming Barriers and Providing Support

With stronger relationships forming, leadership continued to support their team by addressing barriers that hindered collaboration. John, one of the engineers, had expressed frustration with the slow feedback process from the design team, and leadership facilitated a direct conversation between John and Sarah, the lead designer. Together, they worked out a solution — a new communication framework for faster feedback loops. This small but impactful change improved their workflow and created a new level of mutual respect between the teams.

By continuing to address these barriers and providing regular opportunities for open dialogue, leadership ensured that team members felt heard and supported, which further strengthened their relationships.

The Outcome

The efforts to build trust and foster more authentic relationships paid off. Over time, the team at *TechVision* became more engaged and productive. Communication improved, collaboration flourished and team members felt more connected — not just to each other, but also to the company's mission and leadership.

Employee satisfaction rose as individuals felt valued and respected. Innovation flourished as the team worked together to solve problems more creatively and efficiently. And, perhaps most importantly, turnover rates decreased significantly, signalling a shift in the company culture.

The Role of Leadership Expertise

While the progress at *TechVision* was evident, leadership realized that the work they had started was only the beginning. Building and maintaining authentic, trusting relationships is a continuous process, and it can be challenging to navigate on your own.

That's where a leadership expert can make a real difference. A facilitator with leadership expertise can provide valuable tools, frameworks and guidance to deepen emotional intelligence, foster better communication, and ensure that the efforts to build trust are sustainable over the long term.

In this case, a facilitator could help leadership:

- **Deepen Emotional Intelligence (EI):** Gain a better understanding of their own emotions and the emotions of their team, helping to strengthen interpersonal connections.
- **Improve Communication:** Learn to foster open, honest communication that leads to more effective decision-making and problem-solving.
- **Sustain the Culture of Trust:** Ensure that the relationships and cultural shifts continue to grow, adapting to new challenges as the team evolves.

By bringing in an expert to help guide these efforts, TechVision could continue to build on its success, ensuring that the team remains strong, engaged and ready to tackle the challenges ahead.

Conclusion

At the heart of organizational success lies the ability to create and nurture authentic relationships. By focusing on building trust, promoting transparency and fostering collaboration, leaders can help their teams reach new heights of innovation, satisfaction and performance. The benefits of this approach are clear: stronger teams, increased employee engagement and a more resilient, adaptive organization.

For leaders looking to sustain this progress, partnering with a leadership facilitator can be the key to ensuring that the relationship-building efforts continue to flourish, creating a workplace where trust, collaboration and success are not just aspirations, but every-day realities.

Leading Through Storm at Meridian Health Group

Overview

Meridian Health Group, a privately owned network of specialty health clinics, embarked on a major transformation of its patient care delivery model. This shift was driven by evolving patient needs, new regulatory requirements, and increased competition from large national providers. While the operational plan was sound, the change created turbulence within the organization — employee morale dipped, patient satisfaction scores declined, and turnover among frontline staff rose. Leaders struggled to bring their teams along, revealing gaps in their approach to managing not only the operational change but the human transitions that accompanied it.

The Scenario

Meridian's leadership announced the new care model during a company-wide meeting, outlining how it would improve patient outcomes, streamline clinic operations and integrate new digital health technologies. While the operational and compliance steps were well-defined, the emotional and psychological aspects of transition were overlooked.

Symptoms of Struggle:

- Staff felt blindsided by the changes, citing a lack of involvement in planning and insufficient communication.
- Clinic managers were unclear about their decision-making authority, causing delays in patient service improvements.
- Many team members were grieving the loss of familiar processes, workflows and patient interaction styles, but were given no opportunity to process the shift.

Core Problems Identified

1. **Failure to Distinguish Change from Transition**

   - Leaders treated the transformation as a series of tasks to complete rather than a process requiring emotional adaptation.
   - Staff struggled to let go of the familiar and embrace the new approach to patient care.

2. **Unclear Decision-Making Roles**

   - Without defined decision-making authority, clinic managers hesitated to act.
   - This created inefficiency, bottlenecks and frustration across locations.

3. **Lack of Awareness and Presence**

   - Leadership focused heavily on compliance deadlines and technology rollouts, overlooking signs of staff resistance and burnout.
   - Conversations centered on metrics rather than acknowledging emotional concerns.

4. **Insufficient Communication and Listening**

   - Staff reported feeling unheard, deepening feelings of disconnection and anxiety.
   - Communication failed to clarify what was ending, what was beginning, and why the change was necessary.

Strategies for Success (provided by a leadership development consultant)

1. **Apply William Bridges' Transition Model**
   - **Phase 1: Endings**
     - Host a recognition event to honour the outgoing care model and the dedicated work it supported.
     - Provide structured opportunities — such as facilitated discussion groups — for staff to share their experiences and concerns.
   - **Phase 2: Neutral Zone**
     - Create pilot programs for testing new workflows, encouraging feedback before full-scale rollout.
     - Designate "transition champions" in each clinic to serve as peer support and information resources.
   - **Phase 3: New Beginnings**
     - Celebrate early wins, such as improved patient outcomes or reduced wait times.
     - Share patient testimonials that illustrate the benefits of the new model.

2. **Clarify Decision-Making Processes**
   - Update role descriptions to clearly outline decision-making authority.
   - Establish policies that empower clinic managers to make operational changes without excessive approval layers.

3. **Enhance Awareness and Presence**
   - Encourage leaders to practise mindfulness during meetings and patient care reviews to remain attentive to emotional cues.

- Schedule regular "pulse check" conversations with teams, focusing on emotional readiness as much as operational progress.

4. **Embrace Deep Listening**
    - Hold structured listening sessions where staff can voice concerns without fear of reprisal.
    - Use reflective listening to ensure leaders understand both stated and unspoken concerns.

* * *

Outcome

By adopting these strategies, Meridian Health Group shifted its approach to change management. Staff engagement rose as employees felt heard, valued and empowered to contribute to the transition. Managers gained clarity and confidence, enabling quicker, more informed decisions at the clinic level. Patient satisfaction scores rebounded and the organization retained key talent through the transformation.

* * *

Reflection

This case study demonstrates how effectively addressing both the operational and human sides of change can turn a challenging transformation into an opportunity for growth. Meridian Health Group's experience underscores that in health care, where patient trust and team cohesion are paramount, leading through transition is as critical as managing the change itself.

About the Author

Nicole van Kuppeveld is a leadership researcher, author, conference speaker and coach who specializes in helping leaders create thriving, high-performance cultures through her transformational **Feminine-Inspired Leadership ™** approach. She has spent over 20 years researching leadership and applying lessons learned from her work with leaders at all levels. Nicole has held substantive leadership roles and knows how to build healthy workspaces that foster team collaboration, learning and growth.

With a Master of Business Administration in Leadership & Organizational Development and certifications in Myers Briggs Type Indicator and an Advanced Facilitator Credential from the Waters Centre for Systems Thinking, she is a sought-after conference speaker and leadership coach. Nicole has earned the trust of organizations across industries, from health care to post-secondary education, where she led multi-million-dollar initiatives. Through her VIP, Team and Women's Strategic Thinking (coaching) sessions and leadership development programs, she delivers practical tools and strategies to show leaders how to break through barriers, unlock their teams' full potential, and build strong, high performing, innovative cultures.

Nicole lives in Alberta, Canada. She is actively involved in her community and is an executive member of the Women In Business Association (WIBA) of Strathcona County board of directors. WIBA empowers women to become effective change-makers as entrepreneur leaders. Nicole enjoys spending time with friends, family, her grandson, her partner and their rescue dog, Ronan (the Handsome). Nicole is the curator and co-author of *Creating Connections: How Friendships Feed the Soul*, an anthology exploring the importance of cultivating meaningful relationships, something she believes is key to both personal and leadership success.

A few ways you can connect with Nicole and the Organizations by Design Inc. team:

- **Learn more about us**
  https://www.feminineinspiredleadership.ca check out upcoming events or take a deep dive into our learning experiences (programs)
    - Leadership Foundations
    - Building Collaborative Teams
    - Change Endurance Series
    - Leaders! Make More Time
    - From Vision to Impact: A Systems Leadership Journey
    - ELEVATE
    - Building Confidence in Communication for Leaders
    - Women's Leadership Series
- **Subscribe to** our *Feminine-Inspired Leadership* **weekly newsletter** to get more resources, great articles, and stay in the loop about upcoming learning events.
  https://api.leadconnectorhq.com/widget/form/wdiM9e3Dx4YskyiTtKzt
- **Initiate a relationship**. Reach out for an online coffee conversation or strategic thinking session on leadership .
  api.leadconnectorhq.com/widget/bookings/leadership-strategy-session

- **Get more resources.** If you liked the resources toolkit in this book, reach out to info@feminineinspiredleadership.ca there is more to share.
- **Follow us on social media via** @feminineinspiredleadership | Instagram, Facebook | Linktree

For bulk orders or discounts on 25+ copies, go to
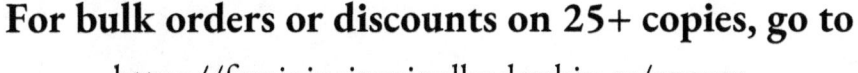
https://feminineinspiredleadership.ca/engage

www.ingramcontent.com/pod-product-compliance
Lightning Source LLC
Chambersburg PA
CBHW072133160426
43197CB00012B/2083